God's Own Junkyard

God's Own Junkyard

The planned deterioration of America's landscape

PETER BLAKE

HOLT, RINEHART AND WINSTON   NEW YORK

Acknowledgments

This book was made possible by a Fellowship awarded to me by the Graham Foundation for Advanced Studies in the Fine Arts; and though the result is hardly a study of the *fine* arts, I am tremendously grateful to the Graham Foundation and, especially, to its inspired Director, John D. Entenza, for venturing into an area where wealthier and larger angels have so far feared to tread.

I am further indebted to Elaine Lustig, who designed this book and translated my intentions into an effective, visual argument; to Arthur A. Cohen, whose editorial suggestions and judgments have, I believe, made this a better book; and to many others who helped by supplying facts as well as photographs.

"Song of the Open Road" is from *Verses From 1929 On* by Ogden Nash, copyright 1932 by Ogden Nash. The poem originally appeared in *The New Yorker*. By permission of Little, Brown and Company, publishers.

The extract from "The Road Not Taken" is from *Complete Poems of Robert Frost*. Copyright 1916, 1921 by Holt, Rinehart and Winston, Inc. Copyright renewed 1944 by Robert Frost. Reprinted by permission of Holt, Rinehart and Winston, Inc.

A small portion of the text first appeared in the May, 1961 issue of *Horizon*, in an article entitled "The Ugly America." I am grateful to the editors of *Horizon* for launching me on my muckraking career.

P.B.

FOR JOHN ENTENZA
WHO DESERVES MUCH MORE

Published by Holt, Rinehart and Winston
383 Madison Avenue, New York, New York 10017.

Published simultaneously in Canada by
Holt, Rinehart and Winston of Canada, Limited.

A portion of this book has appeared
under the title "The Suburbs Are A Mess"
in The Saturday Evening Post, *October 5, 1963.*
© 1963 by Peter Blake.

Library of Congress Catalog Card Number: 63-22178
ISBN Hardbound: 0-03-047431-0
ISBN Paperback: 0-03-047436-1

Designer: Elaine Lustig
Printed in the United States of America
10 9 8 7 6 5 4 3 2 1

God's Own Junkyard was originally published in 1964. It was one of several books of the 1960s that attempted to make us aware of environmental issues—and to make us mad enough to fight for a cleaner, healthier, more beautiful, and more ecologically balanced environment, both natural and man-made. It was provocative, and I remember being quite proud of a phrase in my introduction that said "this book is not written in anger. It is written in fury." Of course it was—it was part and parcel of that emotional period that began with the election of an exciting young president who promised and tried to remake the world; that next had to deal with the nightmare of his murder and the murders of others whom we admired; that then moved from frustration into urgent political resistance to the Vietnam war; and that finally settled down into serious pursuits of environmental issues in the 1970s.

It was a furious book, and it still is. And though I have changed my mind on some of the issues I discussed fifteen years ago, the changes are those of emphasis, not really of substance. I make no apologies for anything I said in my original text—and I have not altered a single photograph, paragraph, or caption.

Before discussing the areas in which I *have* changed my mind, let me make one or two immodest claims: I am fairly proud of having helped, just a little bit, to clean up the garbage all around us. Although President Carter did not request any funds for highway beautification in his fiscal 1980 budget, the laws regulating billboards in most parts of the United States are stricter today than they were when *God's Own Junkyard* was first published, and there are stricter laws governing other forms of environmental pollution. The billboard lobby has lost many court battles, and some of those losses really hurt.

And many parts of this fairly spectacular country have now been returned to Mother Nature—or, at least, to the National Park Service. A tiny, endangered snail darter here and a rare whooping crane there may, today, halt the construction of still another multi-million dollar pork-barrel dam by the U.S. Corps of Engineers and its cronies in the Portland Cement Association. Many barbaric superhighways have been stopped in mid-construction; others, already constructed, are now slated for demolition. Many waterfronts have been restored to people, to fish, to birds, and to ships.

Many streets have been liberated from the tyranny of the automobile and restored to the pedestrian. Cars may no longer emit poisonous exhausts, and no major building project may proceed without prior approval after a detailed "environmental impact study." When I wrote *God's Own Junkyard*, Robert Moses, the New York demigod of superplanning, was still making statements like: "the current fiction is that . . . any busy housewife who gets her expertise from newspapers, TV, radio, and telephone is, *ipso facto*, endowed to plan in detail a huge metropolitan complex good for a century. In the absence of prompt decisions by experts, no work, no payrolls, no arts, no parks, no nothing will move." Today, any such remark would be laughed out of court.

Today, also, a proposal to lay waste to the center of Albany, New York, for example, and to replace it with a neo-fascist assemblage of skyscrapers and paved and windswept plazas would be found totally unacceptable by the citizenry, by the mayor of the town, and by the gov-

Top: *Faneuil Hall Market Place, Boston, Massachusetts. Restoration by Benjamin Thompson and Associates, Architects, was completed in 1978. It is probably the best downtown pedestrian mall in the U.S. to date. (Photo: Steve Rosenthal—Courtesy Benjamin Thompson and Associates, Inc.)*

Middle: *Pedestrian mall in the center of Hamburg, Germany. It is one of many recent triumphs of man, woman, and child over the automobile. (Photo: Peter Blake)*

Bottom: *Walt Disney World, near Orlando, Florida. Its scale and some of its detail have much to teach the modern urban planner. (Photo: Peter Blake)*

ernor of the state. And if the superplanners' bulldozers attempted to move in nonetheless, there would be blood in the streets.

It is obvious that I cannot take too much credit for this change in climate. But *God's Own Junkyard* did make some minor contribution. And I am amazed by the change that all of us in some way have effected: in a mere fifteen years ideas that seemed daring and objectives that seemed absurdly unattainable have become part and parcel of our political and intellectual coinage.

No longer do people have to go to war against despoilers of the environment—the would-be despoilers have to justify their plans, long before the fact; and they frequently lose out.

No longer do people have to go to jail—as Jane Jacobs did to stop the proposed Lower Manhattan Expressway—except, possibly, in New Hampshire: instead, those who try to impose their profitable atrocities upon the rest of us may risk legal action.

And no longer do historic preservationists have to chain themselves to marble columns in an attempt to save a landmark. Instead, those who try to tear down a great relic from our past have to justify their intended act of pat- or matricide in a court of law; and more often than not they lose out.

I do not claim that we have yet reversed the trend toward the uglification of this country. But I do think we have slowed it down considerably. I live on the Boston waterfront, and I have lived there for about four years. During that time some remarkable things have happened in these precincts: the old granite warehouses that stood abandoned when I moved here from New York are being rehabilitated and turned into apartments and stores; the old markets that stood equally abandoned only three years ago are, today, bustling with activity; the old bulkheads that were crumbling when I came to Boston are now being reinforced— and there are now waterfront parks and promenades that may soon rival those of Copenhagen. "The Walk to the Sea"—a phrase coined by Boston's Mayor Kevin White—has become one of the most popular pastimes of Bostonians, whose new frontier is indeed the waterfront, with its historic harbor, the harbor islands, and the ocean—Boston's view to and of the world. Slowly but surely the highway engineers are being frustrated in their efforts to preempt waterfronts for the automobile (and for its powerful backers in labor and industry); slowly but surely those who have been polluting the waters are being forced to make amends and repairs. Any day now, those who risk a swim in the Massachusetts Bay may not have to have their stomachs pumped after the fact.

Things have been looking up not only in Boston, but also in San Francisco, and, to a lesser degree, in New York, Philadelphia, Baltimore, Pittsburgh, and elsewhere. Suddenly our cities—cleaned up, detoxified, and historically preserved—are once again the places where all the action is. The flight to the suburbs, so devastatingly destructive in the 1950s and the 1960s, is being reversed—very slowly but surely.

A lot of people in many different disciplines can and should take credit. And *God's Own Junkyard* may have helped, in some small way, to make us aware of certain environmental values. If so, I am certainly pleased.

Now for the other side of the coin.

About two years after *God's Own Junkyard* was first published, a slim   9

Above: *Boston's answer to the superplanners.* (*Photo courtesy* Architectural Forum)

Right: *Landmark columns "preserved" next to New York City's new Police Headquarters. Construction of the new building wiped out most of the landmark that previously stood on this site.* (*Photo: Peter Blake*)

Lewis Wharf, the first of the old granite warehouses on the Boston waterfront to be redesigned into apartments by the architect Carl Koch. Its reconstruction started a powerful trend in the old city's new growth. (*From* A Pictorial History of Architecture in America *by G. E. Kidder-Smith*)

Facing page: *Another view of Faneuil Hall Market Place, in Boston. Apart from being an enormously successful downtown shopping center, it serves as an effective link between the center of the city and its redis- covered waterfront.   (Photo: Steve Rosenthal—Courtesy Benjamin Thompson and Associates, Inc.)*

Above: *Re Umberto Olive Oil mural, Lower West Side, Manhattan. This rather special façade has now been covered with white paint—and thus, presumably, it has been beautified.   (Photo: Peter Blake)*

volume entitled *Complexity and Contradiction in Architecture* was published by New York's Museum of Modern Art in association with the Graham Foundation for Advanced Studies in The Fine Arts (which had, incidentally and ironically, subsidized *God's Own Junkyard* as well). *Complexity and Contradiction* was the work of a then relatively unknown Philadelphia architect named Robert Venturi; and it made him, almost overnight, one of the most interesting new theoreticians in the area of the man-made environment.

Venturi was and is to modern architecture what Robert Rauschenberg and Andy Warhol are to modern art: he (like they) has pointed out that there are certain resources or manifestations on the popular scene that have been ignored for much too long and that should now be recognized for their potentially invigorating values. Garish billboards, flashing neon signs, and vulgar eyesores on every roadside of the land have become, in the eyes of some highly perceptive artists, a new and utterly unexpected cultural resource: a new pop art, a new pop architecture.

Venturi went well beyond that initial recognition of Pop as an architectural resource. He pointed out that there were certain symbols that had been quite innocently fashioned by people who had very few cultural pretensions; and that such symbols were, perhaps, just as valid as the temples and palaces and obelisks of the past. My photograph of the Big Duck near Riverhead, Long Island, New York, (101) enchanted him— while it bothered me and most of my readers. And Venturi announced that "The Parthenon is a Duck."

"The Parthenon is a Duck."
(Drawing: Robert Venturi)

That phrase—The Parthenon is a Duck—became the rallying cry of a new avant-garde . . . or, anyway, a new pop-garde.

I must confess that I was absolutely stunned—and then vastly amused. Venturi, a man I admire with very little reserve, was not the first one to challenge do-gooders such as myself. Rauschenberg had said, much earlier, that "Times Square is America's Greatest Work of Art"; and in reexamining, in 1979, the photograph (3) on pages 50 and 51, I must confess that Rauschenberg may have been right. And I must further confess that certain photographs I included as examples of God's Own Junk in my 1964 book now strike me as extraordinarily interesting— even beautiful. Specifically, the Army & Navy Store (34) is clearly much more interesting than that Less-is-More-Store on the facing page (Venturi, quite rightly, had written in 1966 that "Less is a Bore"). The Paradise Restaurant (38) is, quite obviously, much more inviting than the Four Seasons; and I must also confess that whenever I drive through Colorado, or Maine, or Louisiana, or any other state of the union with its homogenized highways, I look for the nearest Ramada Inn or the nearest Holiday Inn billboards, with the color TV they promise in every "suite." I don't, in truth, look for the kind of idyllic lodge shown in plate 77—I am usually too tired to do so, after 400 miles of dodging radar.

In some ways *God's Own Junkyard* seems to have provoked a number of interesting polemics. It didn't just (predictably) mobilize the garden clubs; it also mobilized the pop-garde. *Its* members felt that much of what I had assailed was, in fact, not to be sneered at at all! Venturi himself, in one of his most celebrated projects, proposed a "Football Hall of Fame" in the form of a huge billboard that would display to all passing motorists who was winning and who was being clobbered that day. Others, in this country, in Europe, and in Japan, began designing and building junk buildings—ironic comments on the current cultural scene. Jan Wampler, a young professor of architecture at MIT, published a

14

Giant Cigarette Butts, by Claes Oldenburg, were installed on the M.I.T. campus in 1976, presumably by the Surgeon General to alert M.I.T.'s students.   (Photo: Peter Blake)

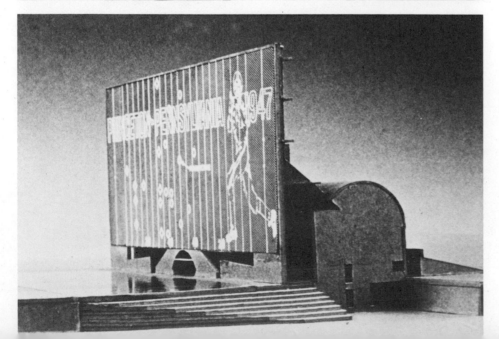

Facing page top: *Times Square revisited. Although its social connotations have become increasingly tawdry, its visual messages have become more and more dazzling.* (Photo: Peter Blake)

Facing page middle: *On the other hand, some of our most highly praised urbanistic beauty parlors seem to have dazzled no one at all.* (Photo: Charles Correa)

Facing page bottom: *"Football Hall of Fame" project by Robert Venturi and John Rauch is a building that is, in fact, a billboard.* (Project: Venturi & Rauch)

Above: *Peeling façade near La Place de la Concorde, Paris. From pop architecture to junk architecture, in (roughly) thirty minutes.* (Photo: Peter Blake)

Below left: The road to Mashhad, in northeastern Iran, where the borders of Afghanistan, Iran, and the U.S.S.R. meet. This was clearly an extreme outpost of the capitalist empire. (Photo: Rondal Partridge)

Below right and bottom: Chandni-Chawk, where all the action is in Delhi, and the Raj Path, carefully designed by Sir Edwin Lutyens, where none of the action is. (Photo: Peter Blake)

book called *All Their Own—People and the Places They Build,* documenting some of the junk architecture that had been part and parcel of the American pop scene for many decades, but that had been largely ignored by elitist snobs like myself. John Habraken, also of MIT, designed and built a house that could be made of discarded beer bottles . . . thus solving at least three problems with one swat: how to increase housing stock, how to revitalize the bottle industry, and how to encourage people to pick up junk. And Martin Pawley, the British architect, published a book considered thoroughly reprehensible by his country's establishment—it was entitled *Garbage Housing,* and actually *celebrated* junk as a physical and visual resource.

Each of these fascinating events did two things to me: it jolted me; and it convinced me that junk had become one of the principal problems in capitalist, consumer-oriented nations. (One cannot imagine that *God's Own Junkyard* would be even remotely comprehensible to anyone in the People's Republic of China!)

Junk, in our wasteful world, had become not only a serious problem, but also a great opportunity; and those who came after the publication of my book—people like Venturi, Pawley, Habraken, and so on—took the next step and began to explore the opportunities—both aesthetic and physical.

And I did also. Judging by the kinds of photographs I began to take on trips after the emergence of the pop-garde, it is clear that I had become less and less interested in established, certified, and acknowledged "Grade A" Architecture, and more and more interested in the potentials of junk, both physical and visual. In Isfahan, that most entrancing city Iranians call "half the world," I was fascinated by a display of used and probably stolen chromium hubcaps on the front of a primitive junk shop, along a dusty highway; and in Delhi, another architectural Mecca, the most intriguing sight seemed to be a vast panorama of unrelieved chaos along what is known as Chandni-Chawk. Clearly, my own focus has shifted considerably.

But not all the way. Many members of the emerging pop-garde in **19**

environmental design have taken the position that if the public wants junk, then—by all means—let us give them junk. Venturi, for example, has said that "Main Street is almost all right," which is balderdash. Main Street, USA, is almost uniformly dismal, disgraceful, and frequently disgusting. He has glorified the Las Vegas strip, conveniently forgetting, I suspect, that the proliferation of highway extravaganzas like vast shopping centers, fast food chains, and similar razzle-dazzle merchandizing efforts have destroyed whatever stores and restaurants the traditional urban street still had to offer—and thus destroyed a significant part of the quality of urban life, including the quality of Main Street—which ended up (as a direct result) not even remotely "all right."

But, above all, it seems a bit condescending to me that highly sophisticated designers and critics have decided that if the public prefers vulgarity, then it is the function of artists and intellectuals to dish out garbage.

The analogy does not quite apply to painting and to sculpture, but it applies to architecture and to urban design. A pop art creation by the marvelously witty artist Claes Oldenburg, for example, may be an ironic comment on the contemporary passing parade—when displayed in a museum—but a pop architecture creation on Main Street merely reinforces the dismal status quo: it is a rather distressing surrender to the kind of Middle American "mystique" on which Richard Nixon tried to build his curious vision. "The artist must be a messenger of discontent," the philosopher Edgar Singer wrote a while ago. The pop architects seem to say that the artist should be a messenger of the Lowest Common Denominator.

At the risk of seeming a trifle pompous, I would like to suggest that the artist must also be a messenger for an ideal. In autocratic societies,

all one needed, in fact, was one Federigo da Montefeltro, Duke of Urbino —and the game was won for beauty.

But in an egalitarian democracy, the pursuit of excellence on every level—from president to plumber and beyond—becomes the responsibility of every citizen, and especially of the citizens who take special pride in their craft. The idea that such craftsmen and artists and other professionals should deliberately abdicate to mediocrity strikes me as a massive intellectual cop-out.

Still, in spite of being concerned about seeing our best talents join the barbarians—and seeing the former exploited by the latter—I must confess that my life has been changed by the new visions projected by the pop architects and their ilk. The great Russian Suprematist painter, Kasimir Malevich, wrote about sixty years ago: "Only that man can be said to be alive who doesn't mind discarding what he believed yesterday." I haven't discarded everything, by any means; but I am open to further suggestions.

PETER BLAKE
Boston, Massachusetts
January, 1979

This book is not written in anger. It is written in fury—though not, I trust, in blind fury. It is a deliberate attack upon all those who have already befouled a large portion of this country for private gain, and are engaged in befouling the rest.

Some of these latter-day vandals are well organized and well financed—such as the billboard industry whose profitable creations along our highways have been implicated in a staggering number of automobile accidents (see p. 12). Some of our latter-day vandals are "little people" —tradesmen and shopkeepers trying to make a modest living—people without ties to the landscape or townscape in which they live, people whose eyes have lost the art of seeing. And still others among our latter-day vandals are all the rest of us—all of us who no longer care, or no longer care enough.

A very cynical acquaintance of mine said to me recently: "The national purpose of the United States, from the very beginning, has been to let everyone make as much money as he possibly can. If they found oil under St. Patrick's Cathedral, they would put a derrick smack in the center of the nave, and nobody would give the matter a second thought."

This is perhaps a rather naïve book. It is based on the assumption that our national purpose, or purposes, are somewhat more idealistic. It is based on the further assumption that it is not too late for us to learn to see again, and to learn to care again about the physical aspects of our environment. And it is based, finally, on the assumption that ours could be a reasonably civilized society—if enough of us could be stirred into action.

This is, therefore, a muckraking book, not because muckraking is a particularly enjoyable activity, but because there seems to be so much muck around that needs to be raked so that this country may be made fit again to live in.

No people has inherited a more naturally beautiful land than we: within an area representing a mere 6 per cent of the land surface of the globe we can point to mountain ranges as spectacular as those of the Dolomites and to jungles as colorful as those of the Amazon valley; to lake-studded forests as lovely as those of Finland and to rolling hills as gentle as those around Salzburg; to cliffs that rival those of the French Riviera and to sandy beaches that are unexcelled even by the shores of Jutland; in short, to about as varied and thrilling a geography as has ever been presented to man.

The only trouble is that we are about to turn this beautiful inheritance into the biggest slum on the face of the earth. "The mess that is man-made America," as a British magazine has called it, is a disgrace of such vast proportions that only a concerted national effort can now hope to return physical America to the community of civilized nations.

Our towns and cities boast many isolated handsome buildings—but very, very few handsome streets, squares, civic centers, or neighborhoods. (Even such rare exceptions as Rockefeller Center in New York, now twenty-five years old, have become disfigured as they have expanded beyond their original limits.) Our suburbs are interminable wastelands dotted with millions of monotonous little houses on monotonous little lots and crisscrossed by highways lined with billboards, jazzed-up diners, used-car lots, drive-in movies, beflagged gas stations, and garish motels. Even the relatively unspoiled countryside beyond these suburban fringes has begun to sprout more telephone poles than trees, more trailer camps than national parks. And the shores of oceans, lakes, and rivers are rapidly becoming encrusted with the junkiness of industries that pollute the water on which they depend.

This seems a strange state of affairs in a nation co-founded, and presided over for eight years, by a great architect, Thomas Jefferson. It seems a strange state of affairs in a nation that has, since Jefferson, produced some of the Western world's most creative architects—H. H. Richardson, Louis Sullivan, Frank Lloyd Wright, to name only a few—and some of its most dedicated conservationists, including another President, Theodore Roosevelt.

These men, and many others like them—writers, poets, painters, pamphleteers—believed that America represented not merely a political challenge, but also an esthetic one: a challenge to preserve (and, quite possibly, to improve upon) what someone called "God's Own Country."

Alas, except for National and State Parks not much of the natural beauty of this country remains preserved. And unhappily those fine National Forests and State Parks tend to do to the landscape what National and State Museums do to painting and sculpture: that is, embalm it. (They tend to "elevate" us on Sundays and holidays, rather than enrich our lives all year round.) However praiseworthy such conservation efforts may be in helping to protect parts of the American countryside, they do little to protect those areas in which most of us live or spend our free time—the areas nearest to cities and suburbs.

As for the preservation of man-made improvements, this is almost non-existent: except for a few isolated structures of well-established historic value (or, at any rate, interest), and a few isolated blocks in some of our older cities, none of our impressive architectural heritage is protected. In Manhattan, the magnificent, nineteenth-century iron-and-glass façades south of Bleeker Street are defaced, demolished, or neglected; in Chicago, the Mecca of modern architects the world over, important structures by Louis Sullivan have been destroyed to make way for more profitable enterprises; in Buffalo,

New York, Frank Lloyd Wright's world-famous Larkin Building, designed in 1904 and honored in every single history book on modern architecture, was sold by the city fathers in 1949 to a wrecking firm for a few thousand dollars; the new owners replaced it with a parking lot.

And so it goes—in St. Louis, San Francisco, Baltimore, Philadelphia, Boston, Pittsburgh—everywhere. When a building—whether handsome or of indifferent quality—has ceased to be a "money-maker," down it comes to make way for a bowling alley or a supermarket.

The total indifference on the part of our city fathers toward this country's man-made heritage was never more clearly shown than when New York's stately Pennsylvania Station, built by McKim, Mead and White, was condemned to bite the dust: the Mayor, a former Chairman of the City Planning Commission (and, hence, a man not entirely untutored in matters of architecture), did not even bother to ask his advisory committee on historical preservation to render an opinion on the significance of the old Station— until it was too late. And then he ignored the opinion of his distinguished committee; for, after all, the committee had no power at all!

"History," of course, "is bunk." History can also be politically inconvenient: the syndicate which desired to replace Penn Station with a mammoth amusement center was not without significant political connections.

Yet it would be unfair to place on the politicians all blame for permitting the destruction of our cultural heritage, or to imply that such acts are invariably motivated by sinister backroom shenanigans. Except for a very small (and generally ineffective) minority, few citizens of our great urban centers really care. On April 11, 1955, that popular mouthpiece of New York the *Daily News* (circulation: phenomenal), published a rousing editorial which suggested that another wonderful relic of America's neoclassic period, the New York Public Library built by Carrère & Hastings in 1911, be topped off with a super-skyscraper so the revenue from millions of square feet of rentable office space thus created would put the city into the black. Not content, however, with advocating one act of vandalism-per-page-per-day, the *News* printed in its adjoining letters column an even more spectacular proposal from an irate reader who anonymously signed him- (or her-) self "Overtaxed." "These city fathers make me sick," wrote Mr., Mrs. or Miss Overtaxed, "raising fares, taxes, and so forth in order to get money. They should chop down the Central Park trees, sell the wood, and then pave the place over. Set up a race track in the northern part, a Coney Island at the south end, and a mambo palace in the center. The remaining space could be rented for parking."

On that memorable morning in 1955, the editorial page of the *News* seemed more entertaining than it had for some time. In retrospect, the joke appears to have been on those of us who thought that New York was a reasonably civilized place. It is true that there is no office skyscraper astride the Public Library (as we go to press); but there is one—the biggest in the world, by God!—astride Warren & Wetmore's beautiful 1913 Grand Central Station, just a couple of blocks to the east. And it is true that Central Park has not been paved over completely just yet, but the bulldozers are at its gates, making ugly noises; and a few forays into Olmsted's preserve have been successfully attempted.

If history is indeed bunk, as our city fathers announce by their actions everywhere and every day, is it really so surprising that most of our fellow citizens show very little pride in their hometowns? Is it really so surprising that they don't care a hoot about what their diner, their parking lot, their cut-rate store, their cocktail lounge, their poolroom, and their movie marquee do to the streetscape? Is it really so surprising that the average citizen, de- **25** prived of lasting symbols of a community, begins to create his own graven images—things of which he can be (perhaps justly) proud?

After all, isn't this a free country? "In the name of culture, in the name of esthetics, whatever that is," said the late Robert S. Kerr of Oklahoma on the floor of the Senate of the United States in March, 1958 (only he pronounced it "ass-thetics"), "it will be a grave day in this country when we reach so high an *ass-thetic* pinnacle that men are willing and able . . . to deprive citizens of their vested rights. . . . What kind of culture [is this?] . . . It is the kind of culture one can find in Russia. It is the kind of culture Hitler went down the drain trying to implement in Germany. . . ." The late, distinguished Senator from Oklahoma can rest in peace; no one has yet succeeded in putting over "ass-thetics" in the cities of the United States. The Republic is safe; it is, instead, our cities that are going down the drain.

"We'll reign like kings in fairyland,/ lords of the soil."   HAMLIN GARLAND

Our cities, however, are not alone. When people talk about the flood of ugliness engulfing America, they first think of billboards—and, more specifically, of the billboards that line our highways and dot our landscape.

The problem was stated rather succinctly by Ogden Nash:

> I think that I shall never see
> A billboard lovely as a tree.
> Perhaps, unless the billboards fall,
> I'll never see a tree at all.

Mr. Nash may have thought that he was exaggerating just a bit. But the fact of the matter is that in Chicago, for example, the local authorities have recently been busy cutting down the tops of trees that interfere with the view of billboards along one stretch of Lake Shore Drive. Even the federal government is anti-tree: any suburban developer who plants new trees between his houses (to conceal the freshly planted telephone poles) will find that the United States government, through its Federal Housing Administration (FHA) appraisers, gives him virtually no credit for his efforts—which means, in effect, that he must pay for those trees out of his own pocket. (Anything that is not covered by the FHA-insured mortgage has to be paid for by the developer; and the size of the mortgage is determined by the appraisal rendered by FHA.) At the same time, however, the FHA *will* give a developer credit (about $300 per house, if his houses sell for $20,000) for something called "sales promotion"; and a large part of "sales promotion" consists of defacing the nearest roadsides with hideously garlanded model houses, billboards, and even sideshows.

There are many other examples that could be cited to show that it is the established policy of various branches of government (local, state, and federal) to encourage the desecration of this country and to discourage those who wish to preserve or (God forbid!) beautify it. Perhaps the authorities should be forgiven; for though every public servant knows that "you can't believe what you read in the papers," every public servant also knows that you *can* believe what you read in the *Wall Street Journal*. And the *Wall Street Journal*, on April 14, 1960, quoted beautylover Burr L. Robbins as saying that "billboards are the art gallery of the public." Mr. Robbins is the President of the General Outdoor Advertising Co., Inc. It is a sanctified principle of our democracy, of course, that a citizen may not know anything about art, but he certainly knows what he likes. Why should public servants listen to Ogden Nash rather than Burr L. Robbins?

It is a good question, and the answer to it (in the case of public servants) is gently prompted by certain tactics employed by the billboard lobby. According to retired New York State Senator Thomas C. Desmond, quoted in the March, 1960, issue of the *Reader's Digest*, the gentle prompting works roughly like this: "[The billboard lobby] shrewdly puts many legislators in its debt by giving them free sign space during election time, and it is savage against the legislator who dares oppose it [by favoring anti-billboard laws]. It subsidizes his opposition, foments political trouble in his home district, donates sign space to his opponents and sends agents to spread rumors among his constituents." Sometimes the beautylovers try a more positive approach: our friend Burr L. Robbins, for example, suggested that since "billboards are the art gallery of the public," his industry might enhance its public image by donating valuable billboard space in cities and countryside   **27** to display huge reproductions of such historic masterpieces as the "Mona Lisa," "Blue Boy," "Song of the Lark," and "Lavinia." Unhappily, this promising campaign appears to have made little headway to date —though it was revived quite recently by one Robert Pliskin, Vice President and Art Director (sic!) for Benton & Bowles, who echoed Mr. Robbins' suggestion and submitted that Rousseau's "Sleeping Gypsy" would make a fine addition to the "art gallery of the public."

The billboard industry is not exactly small potatoes, as any motorist knows full well. Still, the actual figures are interesting: between 1940 and 1960, the industry, according to the same *Reader's Digest* article, "increased its take from $44,700,000 to more than $200,000,000 a year." The principal advertisers during a recent peak year (1957) were, according to the New York *Times*, General Motors with $8.7 million, Ford with $6.6 million, and Anheuser Bush Inc. with $3.6 million.

No one in his right mind would charge that the automobile industry intended its billboard campaigns to help accelerate the obsolescence of older cars; however, this is precisely what did happen, in a macabre sort of way. For it has been clearly established, through careful engineering studies carried out in several states, that highways with billboards experience about three times as many automobile accidents as do highways without billboards. Those who are fortunate enough to survive such accidents are, of course, potential customers for the nearest GM or Ford dealer.

Perhaps this is a thoroughly unfair way of putting it. However, since the results of impartial studies on the relationship between billboards and traffic accidents have been a matter of public record for several years now, it is perhaps not entirely fair of the automobile industry to show such apparent disregard for the safety of its customers.

The trouble is, of course, that the record has not been quite public enough. Admittedly, many newspapers and magazines all over the country have shown considerable courage in fighting against billboards (for, after all, both the users of billboards and the advertising agencies that represent those users are the very people who keep newspapers and magazines more or less solvent). Still, the attacks in the press have been sporadic at best, and generally based upon the late Senator Kerr's "ass-thetic" arguments. Moreover, the Magazine Publishers' Association (MPA) has not always followed the lead of some of its more courageous members: in March, 1958, for example, when the issue of banning billboards from federally subsidized interstate highways was debated in the Congress, the MPA called the proposed ban "economic folly . . . and discriminatory against the most responsible elements of the outdoor advertising industry who have shown willingness over the years to preserve the scenic values of America." (And add some "ass-thetic" values, like the "Mona Lisa"?) Although the question of esthetic control had come up before the United States Supreme Court some four years earlier (and had been decided unanimously in favor of control), esthetics are an egghead issue and will not carry too much weight in America at present.

Highway safety, on the other hand, *will* carry considerable weight with most Americans: some 41,000 people are killed each year on the highways, and another 1.5 million are injured, so that most Americans know or have known victims of traffic accidents. The case against billboards on the grounds of highway safety is strong and well documented.

At the height of the great billboard battle of 1958, for example, Robert Moses (who knows something about highways) stated unequivocally that eyesores along our roads are traffic hazards. He cited a study made several

years earlier by the Minnesota Department of Highways which indicated quite clearly that accident rates were related to the frequency of roadside signs.

Similar studies in other states have produced similar conclusions: in February 1963, the New York State Thruway Authority released a special study by Madigan-Hyland, Inc., a New York City engineering firm, which was based upon a detailed analysis of accidents on the Thruway over the preceding two-year period. The study indicated that "advertising devices" were visible to drivers on only about one-eighth of the Thruway's 1,100 miles of roadway; yet almost one-third of all accidents "attributed to driver-inattention . . . occurred on the one-eighth of the Thruway mileage upon which motorists were exposed to advertising devices." Shuffling their figures around a bit, the engineers came up with the finding that "there was an annual average of 1.7 accidents per mile due to driver-inattention on the portions of the Thruway Mainline where advertising devices were visible, and only 0.5 of an accident per mile for this cause on stretches where advertising devices were not visible."

In short, there were more than three times as many accidents per mile on those stretches of roadway where "driver-inattention" was encouraged by billboards and similar eyesores. This is likely to be an extremely conservative estimate when applied to highways (and types of accidents) as a whole, since the New York State Thruway is, by and large, a well-landscaped and well-protected road, and the billboards visible from it are quite far removed from the Thruway itself. Moreover, the study disregarded all accidents that occurred at interchanges—and every motorist knows, of course, that *level* crossings on unrestricted highways are among the most likely scenes of major accidents—and, also, among the most likely sites for honky-tonk displays.

The billboard industry can hardly plead innocence in the face of such indictments: its own manual, *Essentials of Outdoor Advertising*, which was quoted by Charles Stevenson in *Reader's Digest*, states that billboards must compete for attention with "vehicular traffic, traffic signals or other outdoor designs. To counteract such competition every bit of the poster space must be made to work hard." Where there are no other "outdoor designs" that might distract the motorist (and, possibly, save his life) the billboard industry has a field day. "Away from the crowded printed page and overloaded airwaves," one of its advertisements stated in 1962, "your client's message always gets 'preferred position.' " In other words, you can't help being attracted (or distracted) by a billboard way out in the middle of nowhere—which may be a good thing for the advertiser but, as we have seen, somewhat less desirable for the consumer.

To help the poster space "work hard," as the manual put it, the aluminum people, in 1958, developed aluminum foil posters, using a special sheet with perforations that will get the shiny foil to adhere to billboards with standard billboard paste. What this will do to highway safety at night is a chilling thought. And if that should fail, there are always moving signs. "Motion gets eight to ten times as much attention as a static sign," according to sign-expert Douglas Leigh. "Add light and color and you have the ultimate in an attention-getting device . . . advances in electronics, paints and plastics will open up unrealized advances in the field."

Mr. Leigh will not have to wait *that* long: early in 1963, one entrepreneur announced that he was going to mount huge billboards on barges and tow these around Manhattan Island, presumably to distract motorists on the East- and Westside Highways. (Aerial advertising is "old hat," of course—though it received quite a boost over Honolulu in 1962, when a bright, young pilot named Bob Oliver circumvented Hawaii's anti-billboard ordinance by **29** hiring out himself and his plane to drape advertising signs across the sky.) Soon there will be no need for pilots to take such chances: in 1960, a Mr. James M. Crosby, President of something called the "Unexcelled Chemical Corporation," announced that he had acquired the Western hemisphere rights to a Swiss-developed machine named "Skyjector." This little gadget (cost: more than $1.5 million) will project advertising messages on clouds, as well as "such surfaces as skyscrapers, mountainsides, cliffs and dams." The "Skyjector" is mounted on a truck and uses candle power equal to sixty to eighty giant searchlights! (In fact, one bulb in this infernal machine got so hot that it set fire to a stage when the gadget was tried out in a German theater.) There will be no need to drive the "Skyjector" along a highway to achieve the effect of a *moving* advertising sign: the machine can easily project a message on a small slide over a distance of five miles, and it will then appear (on a cloud, the Continental Divide, or the sides of the Grand Canyon, for example) some *25 million times larger* than the original slide. Presumably the projected image can be shifted around a bit: but even if that problem were to remain unlicked, the illusion of motion could be supplied without trouble, for the "Skyjector" can change slides every five seconds!

Although anti-billboard arguments are, at present, likely to be most effective when advanced on grounds of highway safety, the esthetic argument seems to be gaining adherents. This became evident during the Great Billboard Battle of 1958 referred to earlier, which was fought almost exclusively on esthetic grounds.

That battle was a memorable occasion. It was memorable because it represented the first instance in our history that the federal legislature faced up to the problems presented by the systematic "uglification" of the United States by one single-minded private enterprise. It was memorable, too, because after all the rhetoric had died down, the net result of this valiant effort was a feeble compromise.

What happened, in brief, was this: the Eisenhower Administration had proposed that $40 billion worth of interstate highways be built over the years with federal assistance as an anti-recession move—partly to create construction jobs and partly, it would seem, to create more road surface on which to jam more Detroit-made automobiles. The late Senator Richard L. Neuberger of Oregon, supported by other conservationists, proposed that the federal government should keep billboards off highways constructed with such federal aid. This mild suggestion (after all, only a tiny percentage of all highways in the United States was involved) caused the most frightening displays of anguish seen on Capitol Hill since Pearl Harbor; every Senator and Representative from an oil-producing state prophesied the doom of the free enterprise system.

Among those so piteously affected were not only the late Senator Kerr but also the then Senator Lyndon Johnson, Senator Allen J. Ellender of Louisiana (who, needless to say, saw states' rights imperiled by the proposal), and the late Speaker of the House, Sam Rayburn. Both in front of, and behind the scenes, these beautylovers used every device known to parliamentarians to stop the Neuberger amendment. They received some unexpected help from Senators usually identified with the "liberal" side of that body: for example, Senator Pat McNamara of Michigan, a statesman close to the labor movement, fought the anti-billboard measure because it might have affected the jobs of 50,000 carpenters and sign painters. And in the wings, ever ready to lend support to the beautylovers, were the lobbyists for the billboard industry. Their arguments were somewhat lacking in imagination, considering that those who advanced them were supposed experts in the art of persuasion:

"If our country is to be strong . . . maintain its world leadership . . . better public understanding of the honest principles of [*you guessed it!*] the free enterprise system," said one, sounding a bit dispirited. "An attack on one of our media could be an attack on all," said another, obviously in response to having one of his buttons pressed. "The ladies will be able to find their (parked) cars . . . by recalling under what advertisement they left them," added a third, clearly in desperation.

Still, behind the scenes, the billboard lobby was beginning to play rough. Despite the sorry public showing of its spokesmen, and despite the wide support which the proposed billboard ban received in newspapers and magazines, President Eisenhower (a man of good will, and an amateur artist to boot) could only muster a helpless sigh: "I am against those billboards that mar our scenery," he said, "[but] I don't know what I can do about it." His pessimism was shown to have been justified when the highway bill finally passed the Congress: the billboard restriction had been watered down so that it was left up to each individual state to determine whether or not it wanted billboards on those interstate highways. If a state legislature voted to keep the billboards out, the state would receive a bonus of ½ of 1 per cent of the federal subsidy for its part of the interstate system. (That subsidy, incidentally, is 90 per cent of the total cost of the highway.) If the state legislature refused to vote a billboard ban, it would forfeit this relatively small bonus, but would, instead, presumably benefit from billboard revenues.

Because state legislatures are notoriously flexible when confronted by well-heeled lobbyists, the compromise highway bill seemed to represent, in reality, a victory for the billboard lobby and its allies in the oil, gas, and automobile industries. Oddly enough, the lobby's victory has been far from complete: partly because of mounting public pressure, an astonishingly large number of state legislatures has either acted to ban billboards from these new highways or has expressed interest in the program. In 1961, Senator McNamara, the billboard's friend in the ranks of organized labor, found to his distress that a survey conducted by his own Public Roads Subcommittee revealed that at least 40 states wanted the billboard ban incentive program continued. McNamara tried to keep the results of the survey secret, according to newspaper reports at the time, but the American Association of State Highway Officials made the results public anyway. (It turned out that *no* state had suggested the program be abandoned: Alaska is not eligible because this is an interstate network, and the remaining nine states had failed to respond to the questionnaires sent to them.)

All this is encouraging, though it would be a serious mistake to overestimate the significance of this first, mildly successful attack upon America's affluent uglifiers. When the new interstate highway network is completed, it will be 41,000 miles long; however, there are presently some 800,000 miles of federally aided highways in the United States, and the billboard lobby is permitted to deface every blessed mile of them! In addition, of course, there are millions of miles of state highways and lesser roads—almost every one of them an actual or potential billboard alley.

Still, *some* people in the United States seem to be sufficiently aroused to do battle: on a Sunday morning in June 1958, for example, one or several "persons unknown" sawed down seven billboards along a rather handsome highway leading from Santa Fe to Los Alamos, in New Mexico. This act of terrorism raised a serious problem: since the billboards had been located on Indian Pueblo Land, it was difficult to determine just exactly what law enforcement agency—local, state or federal—should investigate the outrage. While officials conferred for several days to decide the issue, citizens of surrounding areas **31** telephoned newspapers and radio and TV stations expressing support for the terrorist or terrorists unknown. Only two, recorded, anonymous telephone calls expressed disapproval: one complained that the lawbreaker had not cut down enough billboards; the other complained that the terrorist (or terrorists) had frustrated plans of a large group of New Mexico citizens who had scheduled a mass burning of billboards for later in the month. The offender, by the way, was never caught. As the late W. C. Fields put it once, in another context: "It's guys like him that give the West a bad name."

In more civilized states, at any rate, citizens have resorted to less violent (though almost equally effective) methods to get rid of billboards. In Maryland, for example, a letter-writing campaign hastily improvised by a group of garden clubs and local officials of the American Automobile Association infused the state legislature with enough spirit to fight the billboard lobby and to pass effective billboard restrictions for *new* highways. (The old ones are now so thickly barnacled with billboards and similar roadside junk that they will perhaps be condemned as traffic hazards before very long.) In Pennsylvania, anti-billboard partisans have bought stock in billboard companies, attended stockholders' meetings to snipe at the management, and waged campaigns to sway the legislature—no conclusive results to date, but one recent petition was signed by 60,000 Pennsylvanians. In California, Governor Pat Brown said that "when a man throws an empty cigarette package from an automobile . . . he is liable to a fine of $50. When a man throws a billboard across a view he is liable to be richly rewarded. I see little difference between the damage done by these two litterbugs." Governor Brown said this while he was running for re-election (and thus needed billboard space badly); he was re-elected by a large majority. And throughout the country, newspapers, magazines, and TV programs have supported the fight against billboards on esthetic grounds.

All this is gratifying. Unhappily, the evidence before our eyes, every day of the year, in almost every square mile of this country, is proof that the effort, to date, has been almost completely inadequate. There are more billboards—some $1 billion worth—in the United States in 1963 than there were when Senator Ellender feared for America in March, 1958. There are more neon-lit hot dog stands, more garish bowling alleys, more glistening diners, more used car lots, more junk piles. "Yet each man kills the thing he loves," Oscar Wilde once said. Perhaps that is why we are so busy destroying this country.

"The day will arrive when the improvements and comforts of social life shall spread over the vast area of this continent."
HENRY CLAY

The next stop on our scenic tour of the United States of America is Suburbia —anywhere! It might be Suburbia, California, or Suburbia, Illinois, or Suburbia, New York. In our egalitarian democracy, we have achieved the ultimate in making certain that all men are created equal: we have just about empowered a branch of the government, the Federal Housing Administration (FHA), to specify the size and shape of the typical American suburban master bedroom (in which all Americans are thus created equal); to specify the size and shape of the typical family room (in which all American tots crawl around equal); to specify the size, shape and style of the suburban house (in which all American youngsters grow up equal); and we have just about empowered the FHA to specify the width, length, straightness-or-curvature, surface, presence-or-absence of trees, sidewalks, telephone poles, etc., etc. of most suburban streets (on which all American teenagers play equal—at their considerable peril).

The massive, monotonous ugliness of most of our Surburbia must be blamed, in part, on those architects and planners who used to advocate a kind of garden-city development in which each family would have its own plot of land and its own house smack in the center of that plot. One of the leading advocates of this ideal was Frank Lloyd Wright, whose "Broadacre City" concept envisaged one-acre plots per family for most Americans. Wright was, of course, greatly influenced by the agrarian traditions of eighteenth- and nineteenth-century America; and while his proposals reflected those traditions and ideals, they hardly faced up to the desperate problems created by recent population growth in this country (an increase of 350 per cent in Wright's lifetime alone) and in the rest of the world.

What happened to *Broadacre City* (with one-family-per-acre), of course, was that it became Suburbia (with about five-families-per-acre). Yet, despite this rather basic change in density, those who proceeded to practice what they thought Wright had preached made no changes in concept; so that Suburbia today is what Wright himself called, in his later years, "a series of anonymous boxes that go into a row on row upon row," and what others have called "the great suburban sprawl."

Suburbia got that way for two simple reasons: first, because the developers who built it are, fundamentally, no different from manufacturers of any other mass-produced product: they standardize the product, package it, arrange for rapid distribution and easy financing, and sell it off the shelf as fast as they can. And, second, because the federal government, through FHA and other agencies set up to cope with the serious housing shortages that arose after World War II, has imposed a bureaucratic strait jacket on the design of most new houses, on the placement of these houses on individual lots, on landscaping, on street-planning, and on just about everything else that gives Suburbia its "wasteland" appearance. As Senator Harrison Williams, of New Jersey, put it recently: "The Federal Government, directly and indirectly, through the laws it writes, the programs it enacts and the regulations it issues, has contributed more than its share to the ugliness of our landscape."

In fairness to both the developers and the bureaucrats, it should be said that they have certainly produced those "improvements and comforts" which Henry Clay hoped to see spread over the entire United States. Suburbia has more open space, more greenery, more modern kitchens, more gadgets, than Urbia. But all of this, and much more, could have been achieved in in- **33** finitely better ways—better for those who grow up in Suburbia, better for those who must, daily, look at the dreary monotony of Suburbia, and better for those who have to pay for Suburbia.

For the sad fact is that America's Suburbia is now functionally, esthetically and economically bankrupt.

The vital statistics of the suburban sprawl are terrifying:

Some 50,000,000 Americans live in suburban developments.
Within twenty years, another 50 million are expected to move into them.
Since World War II, about 6 million acres of our countryside have been covered with little houses on little lots (and the services that go with this).

Consider now these detailed statistics: Nassau County, New York, which is almost entirely suburban, grew from a population of 672,675 in 1950 to 1,300,171 in 1960—interpreted, this means that in this one county alone some 90,000 additional acreas were swallowed up—almost half the county's land. Irving, Texas, a suburban community near Dallas grew from 2,621 inhabitants in 1950 to 45,985 in 1960—all of them suburbanites, all spread out over some 13,000 acres of newly developed land (and the town is trying to annex another 60,000 acres for additional suburban development). Orange County, in California, which forms a large chunk of Los Angeles' Suburbia, more than tripled its population between 1950 and 1960. And Phoenix, Arizona, moved up from being the ninety-eighth city in the United States in 1950 to the twenty-ninth in 1960—almost all the growth taking place in vast suburban developments that now cover the once-beautiful desert like some sort of skin cancer.

There is not much that we can do about the population explosion that lies at the base of all this; but there *is* something we should have done long ago about the pattern of housing this exploding population. For the suburban pattern that has developed in the United States not only eats up land at a mammoth rate, but is bankrupting most suburbs and is, further, making life there only slightly less intolerable than on tenement streets.

The mess that is suburban America departs from the sentimental assumption, fostered by the early agrarians, that everybody should live in their own house on a small lot. The most common residential "unit" today is a single house of about 1,200 square feet placed on a lot that is 60 feet wide and about 120 feet deep. The house is set back some 25 feet from the sidewalk and about 10 feet from each of the side lines of the property. Because the owners have but limited resources of time and money, they often improve only that part of their lot which represents their "front" to the outside world. These front yards are, of course, unusable for outdoor living because common restrictions against fences rob them of all privacy. The rear yard is frequently neglected, and in any case, it is not really big enough for growing children to play in. The results are palpable: children play in the street; parents spend most of their time maintaining a front garden which they can't use; the community has to maintain long roads and long utility lines to service its strung-out houses; and the suburbs go broke.

There is a better way. It is entirely possible to build 1,200-square-foot, two-story houses on lots that measure only 20 feet wide by 60 feet deep. Such houses would be attached to one another, yet they could be staggered so that each would have a completely private patio space of its own, big enough for large outdoor parties and small enough for any family to maintain without trouble. The "surplus land" thus saved—something like 6,000 square feet per family—could then be pooled to create several large communal parks and playgrounds, each big enough for community offerings or athletic events, each maintained by a small annual contribution from member families. (It is much cheaper to maintain a single large park than hundreds of small gardens; and it is much cheaper for a builder to bypass a hilly and wooded site than to flatten it with bulldozers and to cut down all its trees.) This sort of plan not only preserves much of the natural beauty of the areas that surround our cities but also reduces the cost of roads and utilities and, thus, the suburban tax burden.

The tax burden is growing heavier every week. In 1962, a study by the Urban Land Institute revealed that in one typical Philadelphia suburb land developed for individual houses had an average market value of $40,000 per acre, while land on which high-rise apartments were built was valued at an average of more than $200,000 per acre. (Real-estate taxes, of course, are based on such valuations.) High-rise apartments in Suburbia may not be *the* perfect answer, but they are *part* of the perfect answer, for one of Suburbia's most serious social problems is that it has become a new sort of ghetto—a place inhabited, almost exclusively, by families of just about the same age bracket, just about the same income bracket, and with just about the same number of children. Suburbia has very few single adults and very few older couples—whereas in Manhattan (according to one recent survey) almost two-thirds of all women over twenty are either single, or widowed, or divorced, or separated. An occasional highrise apartment, in the midst of a community of rowhouses or garden apartments, would tend not only to lighten the tax burden borne by Suburbia, but also introduce some variety in population make-up. (It would also add considerably to the architectural quality of suburbia, as we shall see in a moment.)

The Philadelphia study reinforced another one conducted earlier in Stamford, Connecticut, which showed that taxes levied on apartments produced an annual surplus of close to $35 per unit when applied just to the cost of maintaining public schools. The reason is obvious: high-rise apartments, especially, tend to attract young families without children, older families whose children have grown up, and people living alone. Single-family houses, on the other hand, tend to produce four times as many public-school children as do apartment units.

In short, it makes eminently good economic sense for Suburbia to encourage a mixture of building types, if only to reduce the cost of public schools. Quite obviously, it makes just as good economic sense to encourage the concentration of buildings on the one hand, and of open park land on the other, so as to reduce the length of roads and utilities, and the cost of policing or maintaining them.

None of this is theory: it has been practiced for years in every Western country including, occasionally, the United States. Baldwin Hills, in Los Angeles, was built twenty years ago along the lines described above. It is one of the most desirable middle-income communities in southern California.

The wholesale destruction of our countryside is clearly not the inevitable result of the population explosion. It is the result of incompetence and ignorance on the part of those who determine the shape of our suburbs. And it is also the result of pressures from those who speculate with land and who have a vested interest in making buildable land scarce and, thus, increasingly valuable. Under the present system of suburban development, the land speculator has been able to make phenomenal profits: between 1950 and 1960, while the Consumer Price Index went up just a little more than 10 per cent, the price of suburban land rose anywhere from 100 to 3,760 per cent, and the end is nowhere in sight.

All the arguments against suburban sprawl cited above deal with practical problems: how to make Suburbia function better by providing really usable outdoor spaces of different kinds; how to make Suburbia more varied socially by attracting people from different age- and income-groups, and how to make Suburbia self-supporting by reducing its operating costs.

If these practical arguments were heeded, the resulting new kind of Suburbia *might* also be beautiful. It will not become so automatically, for there are more bad architects than good ones, and more hit-and-run developers than developers willing to spend a little extra time on planning and design.

But it is almost impossible—given *today's* controls and *today's* pressures— to create a beautiful suburban community; whereas it would be not only possible but relatively easy to create handsome suburbs if we insisted upon a rational point of departure, rather than a harebrained system developed by bureaucrats and mortgage bankers.

In architectural terms, throughout the history of Western civilization, good communities have been made up of three elements: utilitarian buildings (places where people live and work), which may be entirely plain and unpretentious in character; symbolic buildings (places that form some sort of focal points in a community), which are likely to have a much more distinctive appearance, size, and location, depending, of course, on what they are meant to symbolize; and finally (and most importantly), outdoor spaces of different size and character.

In today's Suburbia, it is virtually impossible to create outdoor spaces of *any* character. Individual little houses plonked down on individual little lots do not form continuous "walls" of the sort we still find along the cobblestone streets of Beacon Hill. Our little houses form, at best, a ragged fence, full of gaps; they face each other across wide streets and deep front yards, so that the distances between them are likely to measure at least 100 feet; and because our little houses are generally low-slung, the "ragged fences" created by them, together with the wide distances between parallel "fences," add up to absolutely nothing in terms of definable, outdoor space. For any "outdoor room," just like any indoor room, depends for its success upon the proportions of height to width to length. Suburbia's streets are "outdoor rooms" 100 feet wide, lined (if you look closely) with ragged walls that may be 12 feet high, and completed at each end by an intersection or, possibly, a fire hydrant. No city builder of the Middle Ages or the Renaissance would have dared to propose anything so ridiculously amorphous; if he had, his fellow citizens would have run him out of town.

As for symbolic buildings, what do we see in Suburbia? It is true that there are probably some churches along the nearest highway. But while the churches of our early New England towns and villages were tall enough (and sufficiently close by) to be visible from almost everywhere, the sprawl of today's Suburbia has pushed the churches so far out that their spires are no longer visible farther than a block away. (The Howard Johnson spire, more often than not, is more visible.) This condition may, of course, be an accurate reflection of today's relative values, but it is also a further contribution to the formlessness of modern Suburbia. One of the important functions of a tall building in any community is to serve as a point of reference, to permit people to find their way about without trouble, much as a lighthouse helps a ship's captain to chart his route.

Suburbia's other "symbolic" buildings are those of the shopping center, which is certainly symbolic of *something*—though perhaps not of anything we would particularly want to symbolize. (Some new shopping centers have tried to become "community centers" in a broader sense, and perhaps there is some validity in this.) Then there are schools, police stations, fire houses and, indeed, somewhere, there may even be a town hall.

The meaning of all this is twofold: first, we do not seem, at this time, to possess the sort of common faiths that shaped cities like Florence (whose only tall buildings were the symbols of religion and of government) or, at least, we do not seem to be very strongly committed to any common faiths; and, second, one reason we are not so committed is, quite clearly, that nobody living in Suburbia (and very few people living in Urbia) is conscious of the physical symbols of democratic government—the one faith we do claim to hold in common.

This is not merely an esthetic problem, or even primarily an esthetic problem, because Suburbia, in its present form, is incapable of generating significant outdoor spaces and is so spread out that its few, symbolic buildings are lost among the forests of telephone poles; moreover, we find ourselves with 50 million suburbanites most of whom are totally disinterested in local government, refuse to participate in it, and frequently don't even know what community (if that is the appropriate word) they belong to. The only local issue that arouses any degree of passion is taxes—and that one tends to generate more furore than constructive illumination.

The physical form of Suburbia is not simply an esthetic issue fabricated to exercise the conscience of a few architects; it is a social and political issue that has considerable bearing on the future of American democracy, for during the 1980's, 100 million Americans will be living in Suburbia.

What sort of Suburbia could be created if intelligence were employed by government, concern manifested by the citizenry, and art employed by architects?

The first thing that would happen if we concentrated our houses in one place and our outdoor spaces in another is that our houses would become "walls"—just as the houses of Beacon Hill are "walls." In other words, it would become possible to create outdoor spaces of many different shapes and sizes: courts between groups of houses, accessible to pedestrians only, where children could meet and play without being endangered. (The reverse of the walled-in row-house with its private patio is, of course, that it provides *privacy*, one of the most precious commodities in any mass society, and one almost totally unavailable in today's Suburbia.) It would become possible to create streets that are really streets, not meandering traffic lanes used indiscriminately as gasoline alleys, pedestrian walks and, in the absence of playgrounds, baseball diamonds. The streets might even have some local stores or restaurants, where neighbors could meet. Moreover, the concentration of houses might make it easier to separate cars from pedestrians by having parking lots or garages within close walking distance of every house.

On the other hand, the concentration of houses in clusters could open up parks and playgrounds next to each cluster—parks and playgrounds large enough to be useful, to provide a strong, visual contrast to the buildings, and to permit the preservation of existing trees and contours. And finally, the concentration of houses could be used to create larger, more formal communal outdoor spaces that would serve as settings for symbolic structures of various kinds.

The mixing of building types—tall apartments as well as low garden apartments and rowhouses—would create a vastly more interesting skyline than the present one of telephone poles and TV aerials. It would also provide points of reference within the community, by which people could orient themselves as they now do in Washington by referring to the Monument.

Such a Suburbia may actually become sufficiently attractive and lively to generate its own industry or business, and to cease being merely a "dormitory" for some nearby metropolis. If this were to happen, the suburb itself would gain immeasurably in variety and color, and the region would gain immeasurably in reduced transportation problems.

These are difficult changes to bring about, because nothing is so immovable an object as a government agency stuck in a rut. It is so much easier for FHA appraisers to "follow the book" and rate a "split-level ranch" (on a 60 by 120 foot range) than to appraise more intangible values such as beauty or urban coherence; it is so much easier for a mortgage banker to process a standard mortgage for a clearly delineated property than to figure out a mortgage for a community parts of which may be co-operatively owned; it is so much easier and faster for a builder to pull out a stock plan, copy it three hundred times, do a routine selling job, and move on to the next town than to get a good architect, fight with FHA appraisers, mortgage bankers, local authorities, salesmen and everybody else to produce something that is just a little—or a lot—better; and it is so much easier for a potential home-buyer to follow the lead of the Joneses and of everybody else and just buy the "split-level ranch"—especially if he is "on the way up," and does not want to seem eccentric.

It is all so much easier not to "buck the trend," especially when the trend, as Anthony West put it, "is up." The only trouble, of course, is that the trend is down: the kind of stratified, anesthesized and standardized society being bred in America's present-day Suburbia is not one to look forward to with pleasure. Nor are the purely practical, economic problems being created in and by Suburbia likely to be solved by inaction and insouciance. There are some pretty terrible things that are happening to our cities, partly as a result of the engulfing suburban sprawl: like the suburbs themselves, our cities are becoming ghettos of one sort or another; and like the suburbs themselves, they are rapidly losing all sense of communal identity.

"Thine alabaster cities gleam undimmed by human tears!"

KATHARINE LEE BATES

Our final stops on this scenic tour of the United States will be some of those "alabaster cities" that "gleam undimmed"—at least in Miss Bates' impassioned "America the Beautiful." Miss Bates was fortunate: she died in 1929 when at least one United States city, San Francisco, still could be said to gleam, and when New York, too, seemed occasionally (at sunrise, and when the fog was rolling in from the sea, and visibility was limited) to be made of alabaster.

Things have changed a bit since then: San Francisco is still beautiful in some spots, but not very beautiful in many others; Charleston, South Carolina, pride of the South, is about 95 per cent junk and 5 per cent charming, historic preserve; New Orleans has about the same proportion of junk to non-junk, but the threats to the Vieux Carré are growing daily; and as for New York—well, we said a few unflattering things about it earlier, and we may say a few more in a moment.

There *is*, as a matter of fact, one American city that does continue to gleam; that city, of course, is Miami Beach—the gleamingest place south of the polar icecap. Alas, its gleam can hardly be said to be "undimmed by human tears." For here, in this glittering collection of our most astonishing architectural acrobatics, the affluent society has finally gone berserk! This is the ultimate junkpile—that mysterious place our television stars must mean when they talk of "Videoland." Here the vulgarians have outdone themselves: if Miami Beach did not exist, the enemies of America would have to invent it. Happily for them, unhappily for us, they can spare themselves the trouble. If only, as someone has said, Miami Beach were as good a lesson as it is an example . . .

With a very, very few exceptions, our cities seem to be headed for a grim future indeed—unless we determine to make some radical changes. That future looks something like this: first, our cities will be inhabited solely by the very poor (generally colored) and the very rich (generally white)—plus a few divisions of police to protect the latter from the former. Second, they will become *primarily* places to work in—places for office buildings and for light industry. Third, they will become totally ghettofied—not merely in terms of racial segregation, but also in terms of usage: there will be office ghettos, industrial ghettos, apartment ghettos, amusement or culture ghettos (like Manhattan's gold-plated Rockefeller ghetto, *Lincoln Center*), bureaucratic ghettos, shopping ghettos, medical-center ghettos. In other words, there will be virtually no mixed uses of streets or of neighborhoods, so that most areas of the city will be alive for mere fractions of each day or weeks, and as deserted as Wall Street on a weekend for the rest of the time.

In short, we have lost, or are about to lose, the most important asset of any successful city: variety. This quality—the great choice available to the city dweller of people, things, events—is, traditionally, the principal difference in spirit between Suburbia and the Metropolis. For this quality, and this quality alone, people have been willing to put up with noise, dirt, smog, congestion, traffic jams, crime, high costs and innumerable other urban irritations; the tremendous variety of choices that the big city used to offer made all these irritations bearable.

When we lose that one redeeming quality of the big city, the big city will go under. Downtown Detroit has practically gone under now; downtown Los Angeles seems to have disappeared without a trace; and other big cities are on the brink of disaster. What is the cause of this cancer of uniformity, of dreariness, of squalor that is making our cities about the most unattractive in the world?

Perhaps the best way to explain the massive deterioration of our cities is to separate the idealistic notions about urban design held by the best American architects and urban designers from the facts of life of the American real-estate game.

There are some 16,000 architects in the United States, and there may be some 500 good (including first-rate) architects among them. This is a more impressive resource of talent than our country, or any other allegedly civilized nation, has enjoyed in recorded history. These good (or first-rate) architects have a pretty clear idea of what the American city might be like: they understand the difference between symbolic buildings (like city halls) and so-called service buildings (like apartments and offices); they understand the difference between spaces devoted to circulation—pedestrian as well as vehicular—and spaces that might be impressive enough in scale to form communal centers; they understand the need for esthetic control of certain building-types—control of building heights, control over facing materials, and so forth; and they also understand the need for the occasional offbeat building—the need for a symbolic structure at the heart of the community; finally, they understand, or have learned, some of the lessons of the history of Western architecture—the need to create cities that will not merely serve the functional requirements of their inhabitants, but will also serve to inspire their citizens to proud communal action.

In short, it has been theoretically possible, for the past forty or fifty years anyway, to build great cities in this country and elsewhere—possible in technological as well as intellectual terms. Since 1920 and even earlier, architects have known, more or less, how to solve the ghastly traffic problems that have strangled or are about to strangle most United States cities—how to separate pedestrian from automobile traffic; how to relate expressway traffic to local traffic; how to relate mass transport to individual-automobile transport; and how, finally, to relate the terminals of these various systems to one another and to the various structures within the city.

All this has been known; all this has been repeatedly, indeed endlessly, advocated by individual architects and city planning commissions; and none of it has been translated into reality. Why?

The reason is, quite simply, that just about the *only* factor that determines the shape of the American city today is unregulated private profit: profit from speculation with land, profit from manipulating land and buildings, and profit from the actual construction and subsequent lease or sale of buildings.

With a very, very few exceptions, the buildings constructed in our cities are built without the slightest regard to matters of urban design. They are built, solely, for the purpose of making a fast buck faster. The laws and codes and commissions that exist for the avowed purpose of helping create better cities are utterly ineffectual, and they are seemingly intended to be so; the policies that govern taxation and financing actually encourage and handsomely reward the builders of bad buildings and penalize the builders of good ones.

This indictment of the forces that shape our cities is no mere rhetoric. It is based on cold fact.

The proof is furnished almost daily by almost every newspaper in the country. Some of this evidence is so familiar that we have become inured to its disastrous implications.

For example: almost every major city in the United States has a planning commission. This planning commission may, actually, have the right to plan —but most of the time, its function is to check on proposals made by private developers and to see whether these proposals comply with existing zoning regulations. If they do, all is well; if they do not, the developer can apply for a "variance." If the developer has the right political connections, the variance is granted; if he has not, he will soon cease to be a developer—and someone else, who does have the right political connections, will come along and perpetrate what his predecessor failed to achieve.

Not many developers really have to apply for "variances," because the zoning regulations in effect in most of our cities are so feeble as to make them almost worthless. In New York, for example, the zoning resolution that shaped the enormous postwar building boom in that city would have permitted the construction of a *6 million square-foot office tower* in place of the bulging 2.4 million square foot tower built in 1963 at Grand Central Station! (Actually, the only limit on the size of the Pan-Am Building would have been imposed not by zoning regulations, but by practicality: if the developer had decided to go beyond 6 million square feet, most of his more valuable floor space would have been filled with elevator stacks.)

So the much-maligned builder of the biggest commercial office building in the world actually showed remarkable restraint when he limited himself to a mere 2.4 million square feet! (His brethren in the real-estate game considered him a traitor.) Indeed, when New York's zoning resolution was finally re-written—after having been in force for forty-five years, and after having assisted in the virtual strangulation and desecration of most of Manhattan during that period—the builder of the Pan-Am Building was *still* under the permissible maximum: he could have built as many as 2.8 million square feet on that same, Grand Central site! No wonder his brethren were pained. . . .

To understand what these figures mean it is necessary only to cite three facts: first, every single planner or urban designer of any note in the United States is convinced that the Pan-Am Building is a massive disaster for Mid-town Manhattan—that it is the giant cork that will finally, and forever, plug up that particular bottleneck. Second, every important realtor in New York City fought tooth and nail against the revised zoning law, and considers the new law (which would have permitted a 2.8 million square foot building) a piece of Bolshevism. And, third, the new zoning law, as finally put into effect (more or less), in 1962, was ready for adoption by the summer of 1950. Its passage was delayed for twelve full years by a combination of real-estate pressure and political hatchetry—long enough to permit the unrestricted construction, during that period, of close to 150 new, massive office towers with a total of more than 50 million square feet of space in Manhattan alone!

So much for the effectiveness of city planning commissions. They do, of course, now and then, come up with master plans. Since they have no power to implement those master plans, no one pays very much attention; and since city planning commissions have limited funds, those master plans are not produced by first-rate architects, but by bureaucrats on the city's payroll. Under the circumstances, it is perhaps all to the good that their plans are not implemented.

This raises another question frequently asked when the shape of our cities is discussed: Who are these architects who design the monstrosities that have sprouted, helter-skelter, on every American skyline?

It is a fair question. Who indeed? The answer is that, by and large, they are the architects who can crank out a set of drawings for an office building **41** overnight, or who can pull a stock plan for an apartment house out of a file drawer. For any architect who takes time to think, to design, to consider alternative solutions, to study the relationship of his building to its neighbors, to argue for restraint—such an architect is a costly luxury. It is not that his fee is exorbitant (or even higher than that of the cranker-outer). It is, quite simply, that the carrying charges on a vacant piece of land awaiting the construction of an income-producing structure are often prohibitive.

It is possible to count on the fingers of your hands the major urban structures in the United States that were designed by world-renowned American architects. In its latest annual survey of the 100 United States Architects with the largest amount of work on their drawing boards, the *Architectural Forum* has no listing for such world-renowned artists as Louis Kahn, Paul Rudolph, Philip Johnson, Mies van der Rohe, Marcel Breuer, I.M. Pei, Minoru Yamasaki, or for the office of the late Eero Saarinen. The list of the 100 busiest United States architects contains only two or three names that would be recognized by any layman in this country, or by any admirer of American architecture abroad. Indeed, it contains only a very few names of men whose work has ever been, or is ever likely to be, published in the *Architectural Forum*.

It is true, of course, that a good building by a good architect may cost more than a routine building designed by a routine architect. But the reason it may cost more has relatively little to do with actual construction costs; the extra cost of such a building is often the result of penalties imposed upon good architecture by public policy.

These penalties take many forms. The most severe penalty is imposed by the land speculator, whose activities are sanctioned and supported by the authorities. The Pan-Am Building, to return to that example, stands on a site measuring 150,000 square feet. Such a site in this general area of New York has recently sold for up to $300 per square foot. (The luxurious Seagram Building on New York's Park Avenue cost only about $45 per square foot of enclosed space when it was completed in 1958.) This means that the land on which the Pan-Am Building stands is alone worth some $45 million—and this without any sort of building on it. (Such fantastic land values are only in part dictated by the laws of the free market; they are actively encouraged, also, by local authorities constantly on the lookout for higher tax assessments and, thus, higher revenues.)

A building on a $45 million site simply cannot, under present circumstances, be a small building surrounded by parks or plazas; it *has* to be a big building with millions of square feet of rentable space. The only way to recoup such incredible land costs is to dilute them by spreading them out over as many square feet of rentable space as one can hope to get away with under the law; and the rents that a builder can charge are, of course, limited to a large degree by the rents charged by his neighboring competitors. The builder of a rental building is consequently obliged by the enormity of his land investment to instruct his architect that the building must contain so many square feet of space, that the space must be of a certain quality (so much per floor, so far away from windows, divisible in this way or that) in order to command the sort of rentals necessary to repay the cost of the land, and that the cost of the structure must be kept to a minimum so as to help offset the high cost of the site.

All this means that the architect is placed in a strait jacket tailored by the land speculator. Very, very few architects are able to produce even a moderately decent building under such circumstances, and very, very few builders are able to afford one.

The land speculator is able to operate the way he does because the zoning laws of our cities seem designed deliberately to encourage him. If they were strict enough to limit the bulk of our buildings and thus enable architects to create open spaces as well as enclosed cubage, the market value of urban land would automatically go down—for the obvious reason that no one in his right mind would then buy land at $300 a square foot, or even at a fraction of that price. In other words, the land speculator is completely within his rights, given the sort of economic system in which we operate; moreover his rights are further legitimized by public policy.

The next penalty imposed upon good architecture by officialdom has to do with financing and taxation. Many of the buildings constructed in our cities are put up under some sort of program of local, state, or federal aid. These programs have much to recommend them. Since buildings are considered purely as investments, they must compete for investment capital with other investment opportunities. But other investment opportunities are infinitely more liquid than real estate—they can be turned into cash with no more trouble than it takes to make a telephone call. Buildings cannot; and so, in order to attract investment capital, buildings must offer higher returns, or greater security than stocks or bonds. Or perhaps both.

To make investment buildings more attractive to potential investors, various governmental agencies have developed programs that insure mortgages, or provide loans at low interest rates, or offer some sort of tax abatement. In return for this assistance, the agency concerned establishes standards of planning and design that will, in the agency's view, assure the quality of the building—at least as an investment, if not as architecture.

This means, in effect, that buildings directly or indirectly subsidized by governmental agencies tend to end up being designed by bureaucrats, not architects. We have seen what the rigid, bureuacratic policies of the FHA have done to Suburbia; in cities, these same policies have been almost as disastrous: in various ways, the FHA policies determine how many rooms—and what sort of rooms—American apartment dwellers should inhabit. Among the ridiculous products of this particular bureaucratic effort are apartment buildings full of balconies—in Alaska! (Balconies are considered rooms, or semi-rooms, by FHA appraisers; and since balconies are cheaper to build than real rooms, builders can get more favorable appraisals from FHA if they stick balconies on their buildings.) There are innumerable other regulations that impose additional strait jackets upon architects and builders alike.

Still, once in a while, an adventurous builder will try to break the bureaucratic mold and employ a first-rate architect. What happens? The builder spends interminable months, if not years, arguing with the responsible bureaucrats; meanwhile, he pays taxes for his land, without receiving any income from it; and his capital, which might have earned some interest had it been deposited in the local piggy bank, earns nothing at all. Result: the builder goes bankrupt, other builders are taught a lesson (*stick to routine design*), and the local FHA appraisers are confirmed in their stubborn opinion that any building that is "different" is economically unsound. Needless to say, these same lessons rub off on local mortgage bankers and influence all buildings not subsidized in some way by public authorities.

Privately financed structures are subject to the same sort of pressures: if a builder decides to construct an office tower (and wants to finance it in a "conventional" way), he may form a syndicate and sell shares to the public, or borrow the money from a bank. The public, or the bank, of course, wants to see a return on the investment as soon as possible; so there is no time to **43** "waste" on new architectural ideas, no time to "waste" arguing for new materials (with building-code officials) or for new site-planning concepts (with the planning commission) or for new kinds of rental spaces (with the rental agents) or for new structural concepts (with the general contractors). All you have time for, in fact, is putting up the same old thing—then moving on to the next.

In a curious way, the federal government, for the past decade or so, has actively encouraged such sloppiness by its special tax regulations governing real-estate syndicates. These regulations permit something called "accelerated depreciation," which means that an office building, for example, can be depreciated faster in its early years than in its later years. The result of this interesting little gimmick is that a syndicate that has built a big office building can "write off" most of the cost of this building in the first seven or eight years after completion—so that it becomes most advantageous to the syndicate to sell the building after seven or eight years and let the next owner start the same "accelerated depreciation" process all over again.

This gimmick was introduced as an anti-recession move, by the Eisenhower Administration in 1954, to stimulate more speculative construction. It certainly worked. But from the point of view of architectural quality, the gimmick proved disastrous, for it wiped out the one remaining incentive to a good building: pride of ownership. All of a sudden, an owner was rewarded for selling out fast! The cheapening of the American skyline was noticeably accelerated.

It might seem that these mountainous obstacles to good architecture would suffice to assure the desecration of every American city: exorbitant land costs openly encouraged by local authorities, bureaucratic strait jackets on all buildings directly or indirectly financed by governmental agencies, and federal tax gimmicks so designed as to discourage all pleasure and pride of ownership. These contributing factors seem perfectly adequate to assure this country of continued urban mediocrity.

Apparently not. For we now boast additional penalties on good architecture: if everything else fails, and if a rare, idealistic owner (say a corporation building its own headquarters) should overcome all these obstacles and proceed to commission a first-rate architect to design and build a first-rate building, the city—thus enhanced—will crack down with all the tax power at its command to teach the offenders a lesson they will not easily forget.

It has long been axiomatic in this and other countries that a slum landlord who does nothing to fix up his tenement building is rewarded with a low tax assessment; but that a slum landlord who spends some money to improve his tenement is punished by having his taxes hiked sky-high. Undoubtedly, the laudable purpose behind this brilliant administrative maneuver is to keep people out of slums.

But now the city fathers of New York, for example have come up with a new device: they have decided to put an extra tax on architectural quality! Not long ago, the accountants for the Seagram Building discovered to their surprise that the City was taxing their building at a rate about 50 per cent higher than that applied to the junky, speculative office buildings that have gone up north and south of it during the past years. The City explained this astonishing procedure by saying, in effect, that Seagram was a "prestige building," that it had cost more than the speculative cubage nearby, and that Seagram ought to pay more in taxes for the good will generated by its lovely bronze and glass tower.

Seagram's attorneys went to court to fight this piece of official idiocy, but they found no support whatsoever. In two separate rulings, the New York

State Supreme Court and its Appellate Division upheld the City. And to make quite certain which side the Supreme Court judges were on, they stated that, in their view, the high cost of the Seagram Building "does not do much credit to the sagacity of the corporate mangers." In other words, the corporate managers would have performed creditably had they simply added another pile of junk to the disintegrating skyline of Park Avenue. Not content with having made one culturally illiterate observation, the judges, on the same day, added that the Seagram Building was a manifestation of Veblen's Doctrine of Conspicuous Waste. "It might more realistically be described as an example of restraint," wrote the editors of the *Architectural Forum*, "Who are these judges to set the . . . architectural standard at the lowest going?"

This, then, is the death blow to urban design in America's largest city.

What we have described are, unfortunately, the realities of urban design—the *real* forces that shape our cities. It is true that there are some buildings not built for profit, such as governmental or institutional structures. Occasionally, these buildings or groups of buildings are well designed; but the economic and administrative structure of our cities tends to force them into ghettos of one sort or another, so that they become islands in the townscape without relation to the rest of the city.

The "ghettofication" of our cities referred to earlier is a reflection of a widespread tendency in our national life: the growing specialization of people and authorities. Just as this specialization has tended to create monotonous social cliques within our population, so it has produced monotonous enclaves in our cities, as well as unrelated "solutions" to urban design problems that need to be solved as integral parts of an over-all scheme of things.

To illustrate the disastrous results of this sort of specialization in urban design it is necessary only to mention a few examples: expressway planning, park planning, school planning, civic-center planning, and public housing.

Our cities, like those of other highly industrialized nations, are plagued by one particular, maniacal specialist—the highway planner. In the United States, the highway planner has succeeded in destroying almost every city in which he has been active. One of his standard devices is to build his Chinese Walls along the water fronts of our cities, thus making it impossible for the citizens to enjoy one of the potentially most beautiful assets of the townscape. Almost every civilized city in Western Europe has a water front dedicated to its inhabitants. To list only a few, Copenhagen, Stockholm, London, Paris, Zurich, Florence and Naples have water fronts that are a delight to the eye and a relief on hot summer days. American cities have six- or twelve-lane highways instead. It is entirely possible that some of our cities fronting the Atlantic, the Pacific, or the Gulf have more water frontage than Venice; alas, there is no way of finding out, unless one is airborne.

The explanation for this piece of "mal-planning" is that highway experts rarely if ever talk to city planners—or to anyone else, for that matter. To remedy the disastrous mistakes made by these specialists we are now forced to build whole sections of cities on elevated platforms that can be made to project out over the coastal expressway so as to offer a glimpse of those simple pleasures—a tugboat, a tanker, a liner, or a sea gull. Apparently our highway planners never thought of what they were doing to the city as a whole; all they seem to consider is how many cars they could move—to where?

To where, indeed! For the next example of highway-planning-with-blinders-on is that, having built highways up to the edges of our cities and beyond, highway planners just dumped the cars at the nearest exit and forgot about **45** the whole thing. Or, else, they brought them right into the heart of the city, to add to the existing traffic jams and to force the pedestrian underground. (The latter is the forgotten man of the space age; most of our big, new, urban centers thoughtfully provide him with subterranean concourses so as to make more room for cars above.) Highway engineers may yet succeed in wiping out pedestrians altogether: they are busy surrounding almost every public park, civic or cultural center with labyrinths of concrete spaghetti which appear diabolically calculated to prevent the terrified pedestrian from entering them and have the effect as well of turning motorists into whirling dervishes. Sidewalks are, of course, almost passé; and on the fringes of our cities, where parking lots abound and adjoin the public highway, the asphalt extends as far as the eye can see, and the cars spill over the edges of the highway and into the townscape.

And when the highways are clogged up and all traffic has come to a permanent halt, the proffered solution, as may be imagined, is more highways!

The highway expert would appear to be in cahoots with the park planner, although in fact they hardly communicate at all. The park planner puts his parks where there are no people—or, at least, where there are no people who would want to use the park, or where (if they were there, and did want to use it) they could not reach it, because it is surrounded, and often bisected, by highways.

The school planner is even more cunning: he locates his schools where there are no children! (Several federally supported urban-renewal projects of fine design are on the skids, financially, because while one type of planner was suggesting that facilities be built to house lots of families with children, no school planner ever got this particular message—and so there are no schools nearby.) In any event, the boundaries of a school district have very little to do with the boundaries of any other type of administrative district, so that there is apparently no need for the school planner to talk to any other kind of planner in his general area. (Lest there be any suspicion that these specialized planners are narrow-minded in their approach to their problems, it should be pointed out that all highway planners like to attend highway-planning conventions—at which they talk to other highway planners; that all park planners like to attend park-planning conventions; and that all school planners like to attend school-planning conventions.)

Finally, there are the planners of civic and cultural centers, who have a passion for concentrating all *their* buildings in one tight, little, administratively efficient enclave; and there are the planners of public housing, who have a passion for concentrating all *their* buildings in another tight, little, administratively efficient enclave—this one with an almost visible sign on it, saying: "Everybody living in this ghetto earns less than $3,000 a year." That is, of course, one way of keeping the lower classes in their places. As Dr. Kenneth B. Clark, professor of psychology at the College of the City of New York put it recently: "In its essence, the ghetto is a compound of despair, inertia, apathy, seething frustration, latent turbulence and chronic covert, and occasional overt violence."

Whether intentionally or not, Dr. Clark was describing not merely the racially segregated residential areas of our cities; he was describing the American townscape as a whole. Despair, inertia, apathy, seething frustration and latent turbulence—all these, plus a massive accretion of ugliness that sometimes defies belief—this is the image of our "alabaster cities" today.

1

2

Townscape

The two American scenes shown on the opposite page document the decline, fall, and subsequent disintegration of urban civilization in the United States. The two examples are separated by a mere 140 years in time, and by only a few hundred miles in space: at the top, Thomas Jefferson's campus for the University of Virginia, in Charlottesville, started in the 1820's; below, Canal Street, the busiest business street in New Orleans, as it appears in the 1960's.

Jefferson's serene, urban space has been called "almost an ideal city—unique in America, if not in the world." Canal Street, one fervently hopes, has not been called anything in particular in recent times. It is difficult to believe that these two examples of what a city might be were suggested by the same species of mammal, let alone by the same nation. Jefferson called his campus "an expression of the American mind"; New Orleans' Canal Street, and all the other dreary Canal Streets that defile America today, have not been called "expressions of the American mind" by any but this nation's mortal enemies.

On the next several pages are further portraits of the American city today—portraits, not caricatures. They need no identification; for these are the places two-thirds of us call "home." We walk or drive through them each day; this is where we work, shop, and are also born, exist, and die. What manner of people is being reared in these infernal wastelands?

One answer is: people who no longer see. Recently, the Honorable Mario Cariello, President of the Borough of Queens, one of the five boroughs of New York City, delivered himself of the considered opinion that his Borough "truly represents the full flowering of advanced, urban living." Oh Mario, son of Rome—and of Florence, Siena, Venice, Pisa, possibly even Orvieto—there was once another son of Italy, a man called Leon Battista Alberti, who asked, "How are we moved by a huge, shapeless, ill-contrived pile of stones?" Alas, he lived and died before there was a fully flowering Borough of Queens; and so you may never know his answer.

"Architecture is the masterly, correct, and magnificent play of masses brought together in light."
LE CORBUSIER

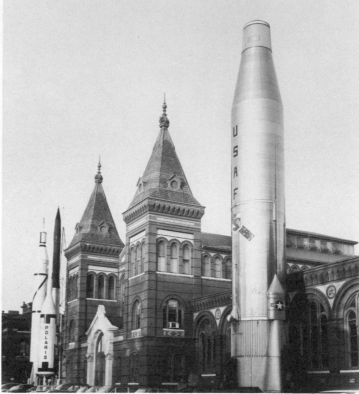

"*America has never forgotten and will never forget the nobler things that brought her into being and that light her path.*"
BERNARD M. BARUCH

9

"*Thanks to our symbols, we are nourished by other lives that have flourished and faded . . .*" LEWIS MUMFORD

"When skill and love work together, expect a masterpiece." JOHN RUSKIN

13

"My God, I shot the wrong architect!" HARRY THAW

"Variety of Uniformities makes compleat Beauty." SIR CHRISTOPHER WREN

*"Beauty is the
promise of Function."*
HORATIO GREENOUGH

21

22

23

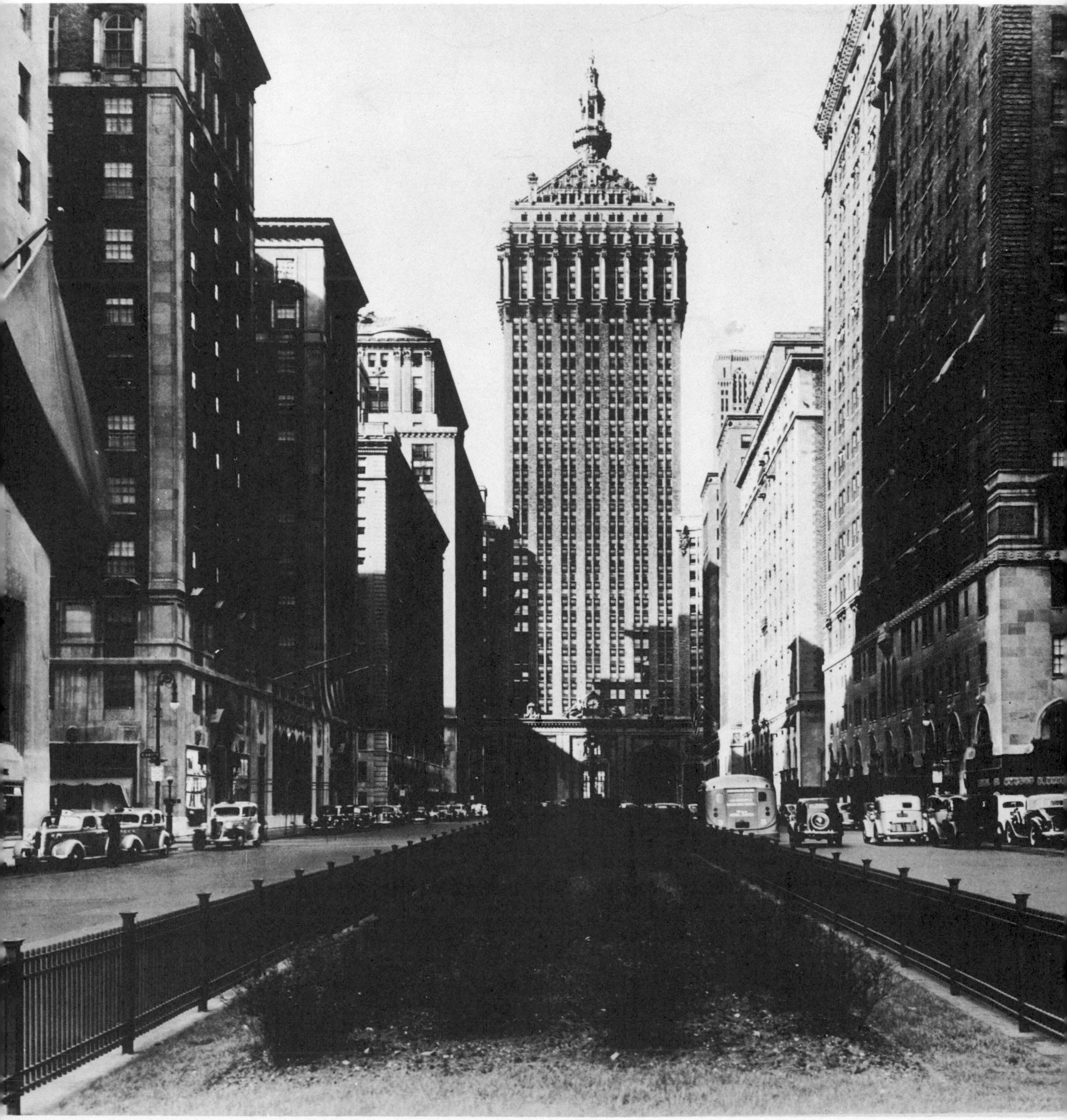

*"I will build a motor car for the great multitude
... so low in price that no man ... will be unable
to own one—and enjoy with his family the blessing
of hours of pleasure in God's great open spaces."*
HENRY FORD

"The American system (is one) of rugged individualism." HERBERT HOOVER

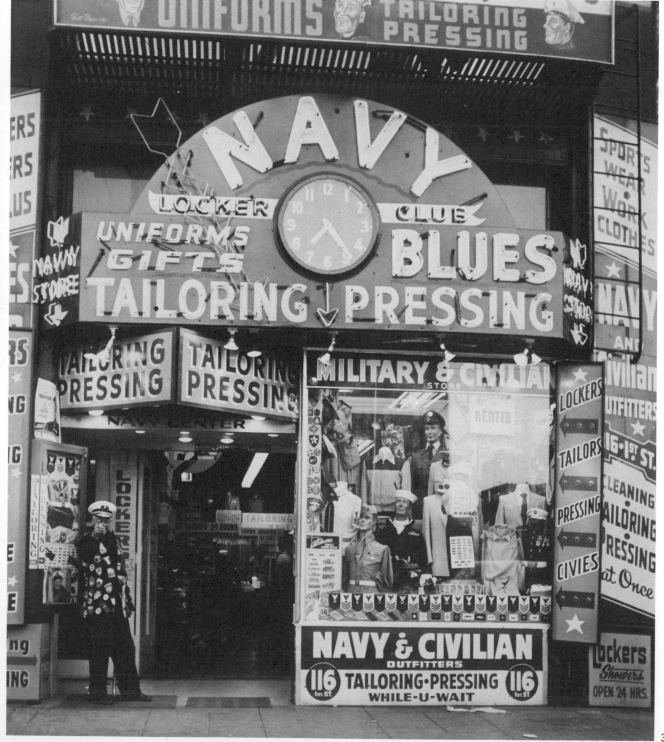

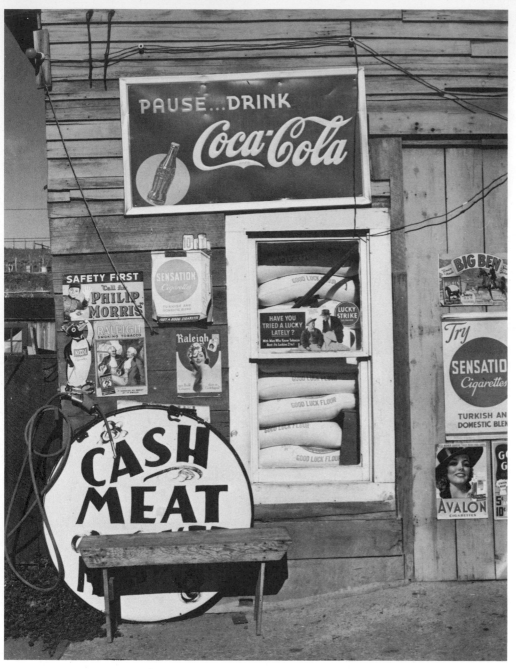

"Never was average man, his soul, more energetic, more like a God." WALT WHITMAN

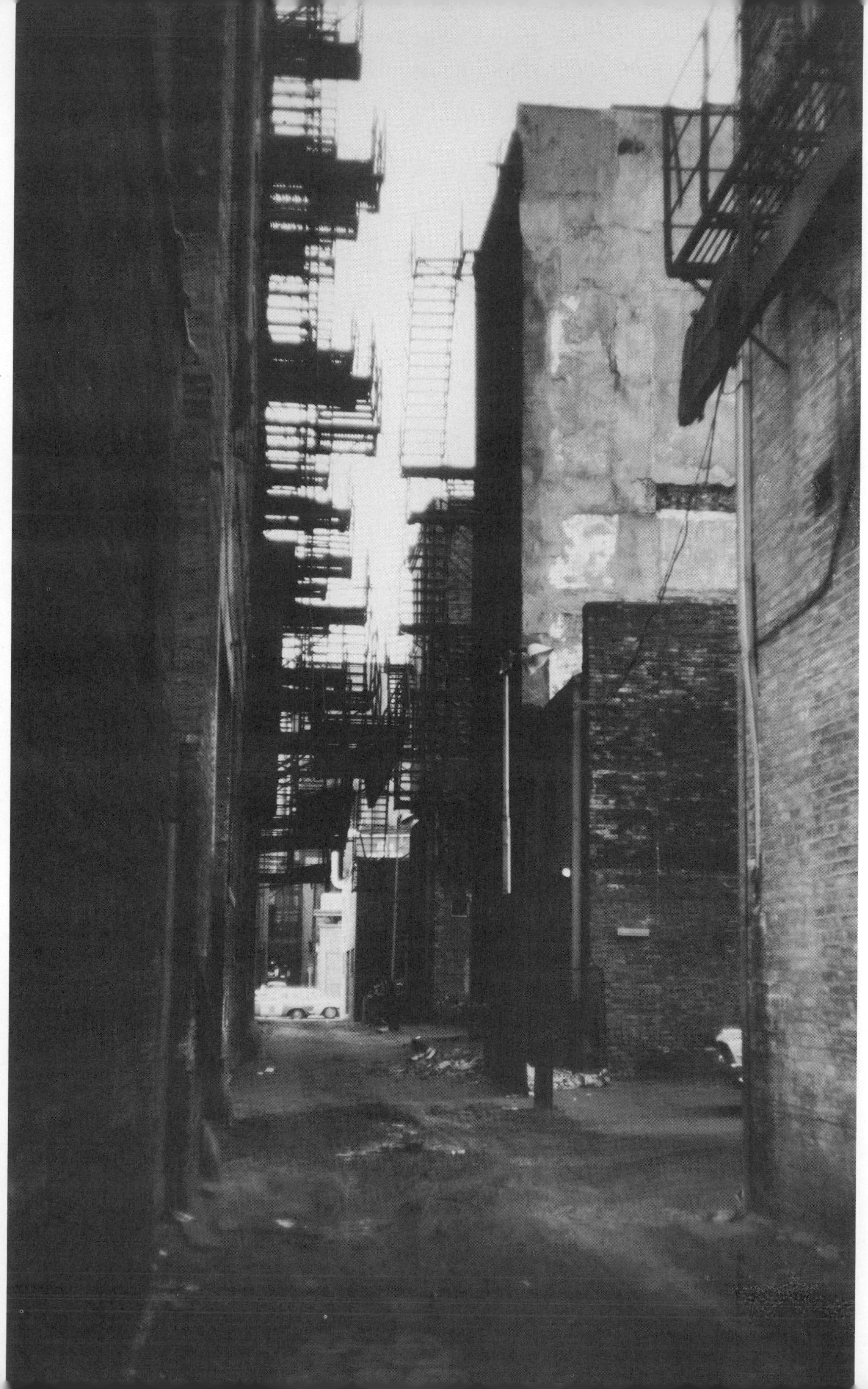

"Let every street be made a reverent aisle
Where Music grows and Beauty is unchained."
VACHEL LINDSAY

45

46

Landscape

There are several ways of looking at our land: there is the choked-up way ("America the Beautiful"); there is the socio-political way ("The land, the earth God gave to man for his home . . . should never be the possession of any man, corporation, (or) society . . . any more than the air or water," as Abraham Lincoln put it); and then there is the point of view graphically stated on the opposite page.

It is a point of view that enjoys the sanction of all right-thinking people, of both major political parties, of chambers of commerce and of labor unions: after all, doesn't an owner have the right to do with his land as he pleases (more or less)? If he wants to cut down all the trees, plant billboards and telephone poles, bulldoze the hills into oblivion, turn the place into a village dump, or chop it up into what one California developer calls "ranchettes"—well, isn't that *his* business and isn't this a free country and what right has anyone to try and stop him?

One answer was given by Tom Paine: "Men did not make the earth," he said, implying that we held it in trust for the God who did. "The land is Mine," God had said to Moses. (Lev. 25:23) "Ye are strangers and sojourners with Me." Though we have established the right of individuals to own pieces of land, the implication has always been that this was a trust—not an absolute right. And judging by the manner in which that trust has been abused by many of its present, private owners, a review of this arrangement may be in order. After all, no one has the right to own the American air or the American waters; some have been given permission to *use* these natural resources, and the manner of such uses has been very strictly circumscribed.

The brutal destruction of our landscape is much more than a blow against beauty. Every artist, scientist, and philosopher in the history of mankind has pointed to the laws of nature as his greatest source of inspiration: without the presence of nature, undisturbed, there would have been no Leonardo, no Ruskin, no Nervi, no Frank Lloyd Wright. In destroying our landscape, we are destroying the future of civilization in America.

"The earth gives us back our animal nature." PAUL GAUGUIN

"We are old hands at starting with the gleam-in-your-eye and finishing with just the sign you seek."
THE ARTCRAFT STRAUSS SIGN CORP.

60

61

69

70

71

72

77

"*(Architecture) must without doubt be directed by some sure rules of art and proportion, which whoever neglects will make himself ridiculous.*"
LEON BATTISTA ALBERTI

"Nature is right, but man is straight." HENRY DAVID THOREAU

83

84

"*. . . but as nothing other than
Part of a benignant plan;
Proof that earth was made for man.*"
THOMAS HARDY

86

87

"The world will little note nor long remember what we say here; but it can never forget what they did here ..."
ABRAHAM LINCOLN

91

92

"I think I could turn and live with animals, they're so placid
and self-contain'd,
I stand and look at them long and long."
WALT WHITMAN

100

99

Roadscape

"Oh highway . . . you express me better than I can express myself!" When Whitman wrote these lines, they held none of the irony they hold for us, the contemporaries of New Jersey's Route 22. The Open Road was then the great American theme—the theme of an expanding nation, opening up a marvelous, new continent.

The Open Road is still a great American theme, picked up in our day by writers like Jack Kerouac. But today the American highway has become the prime symbol of a nation frantically running around in circles and, in so doing, scattering debris in all directions of the compass.

Admittedly, we still possess a few highways that express what is best about America. But most of them are hideous scars on the face of this nation—scars that cut across mountains and plains, across cities and suburbs, poisoning the landscape and townscape with festering sores along their edges. And as these highways cut across our cities, they form massive walls that mutilate our communities by chopping them up into disconnected bits and pieces. On these pages are some of the highways that, unfortunately, appear to express us better than we can express ourselves.

Why have we permitted this outrage? Why do we continue to permit it?

The reason—the *real* reason—is, of course, that Detroit needs more highways to sell more cars, and America needs Detroit to sell more steel, aluminum, rubber, and oil. If it ever became necessary to pave over the entire country to keep Detroit humming, Congress would at least consider appropriating enough money to do just that.

No force is more irresistible than a bevy of "experts" backed by a powerful lobby; and no more powerful combination exists than that of the highway expert backed by Detroit. To this Juggernaut, the ragged little band of all-the-rest-of-us is a pushover. ("All-the-rest-of-us," incidentally, includes quite a few real experts—people who have known for years how to build cities for those who live in them, rather than for cars.) Still, all-the-rest-of-us have proved to be a pushover; and it seems entirely appropriate that in Rockefeller Center, built by oil-and-gas money, the pedestrians have been forced underground, into tunnels, so as to free the land surface for more automobiles.

111

112

"The idea of progress remains a reasoned conviction, a hope that may be realized, is indeed in process of realization."
CHARLES A. BEARD

THE SEAL OF EXCELLENCE

SUPERIOR
COURTS UNITED
INC.

LUCKY FOR THE TRAVELER

THE MEMBER
Diners'
CLUB

RECOMMENDED ★ BY
Duncan Hines
VACATION
GUIDE
Approved 1958

APPROVED
AAA
MOTEL

TANGIERS
MOTEL
AIR CONDITIONED
PRIVATE POOL & BEACH
KITCHENETTES
ROOMS COFFEE
VACANCY SHOP
COCKTAIL
LOUNGE

WAIKIKI

Tangiers
FREE PARKING

ENTRANCE
Tangiers
18695 MOTEL

AAA

ENTRANCE

Tangiers

18695 →

MOTEL

"*Two roads diverged in a yellow wood
And sorry I could not travel both . . .*"
ROBERT FROST

*"Ten thousand leaves on every tree,
And each a miracle to me."*
JOAQUIN MILLER

121

Carscape

As this is written, there are some 180 million people in the United States, each occupying about 2 square feet of our land surface; there are also close to 70 million private automobiles in the United States, each occupying about 120 square feet of land. (In addition, there are 15 million trucks and buses.)

In short, only 360 million square feet of America are being used (at any given moment) by people; but 8.4 *billion* square feet of this country, or 23 times as many square feet, are covered with private automobiles. And if you assume that half of our cars are occupied (at any given moment) by the national average of 1.5 persons per car, then the ratio shifts from 23 to 1, to nearly 33 to 1 in favor of the cars!

For this reason, a reapportionment of rights, privileges, powers, and representation has been brought about in the United States. Facilities in the countryside, in suburbs and in cities are being reallocated so as to correspond more realistically to the respective space requirements of people and of cars.

As suggested elsewhere in this book, the first move in this reallocation of space was to try and pave over the entire country; after that, it was decided to put pedestrians underground, into so-called concourses, to make more room for cars on the surface of our land; and the final step is likely to be to put living and working areas for human occupancy either up in the air or underground, since the ground level will soon be entirely occupied by cars.

This may seem a trifle exaggerated, but it really is not: in a good many cities throughout the United States, apartments have been built on "air rights" rather than real land, because the real land is, of course, occupied by highways; in Chicago, some apartments have been built on top of more than a dozen floors of parking space, so that human beings have to perch precariously on balconies 60 floors up in the air where, in Chicago and elsewhere, it tends to be windy; and in some cities, office spaces, schools and factories are being put partly underground so as not to clutter up the carscape with human beings. (America, in short, is no longer landscape or townscape, but simply carscape.)

And if everything else fails, there is always the solution offered by Commandant Jacques-Yves Cousteau, the French explorer. "Sooner or later," he said, "man will live under water and build towns there." If so, we will at least not have to worry about the dangers of air pollution.

"In the United States there is more space
where nobody is than where anybody is.
This is what makes America what it is."
GERTRUDE STEIN

122 | 123
124 | 125

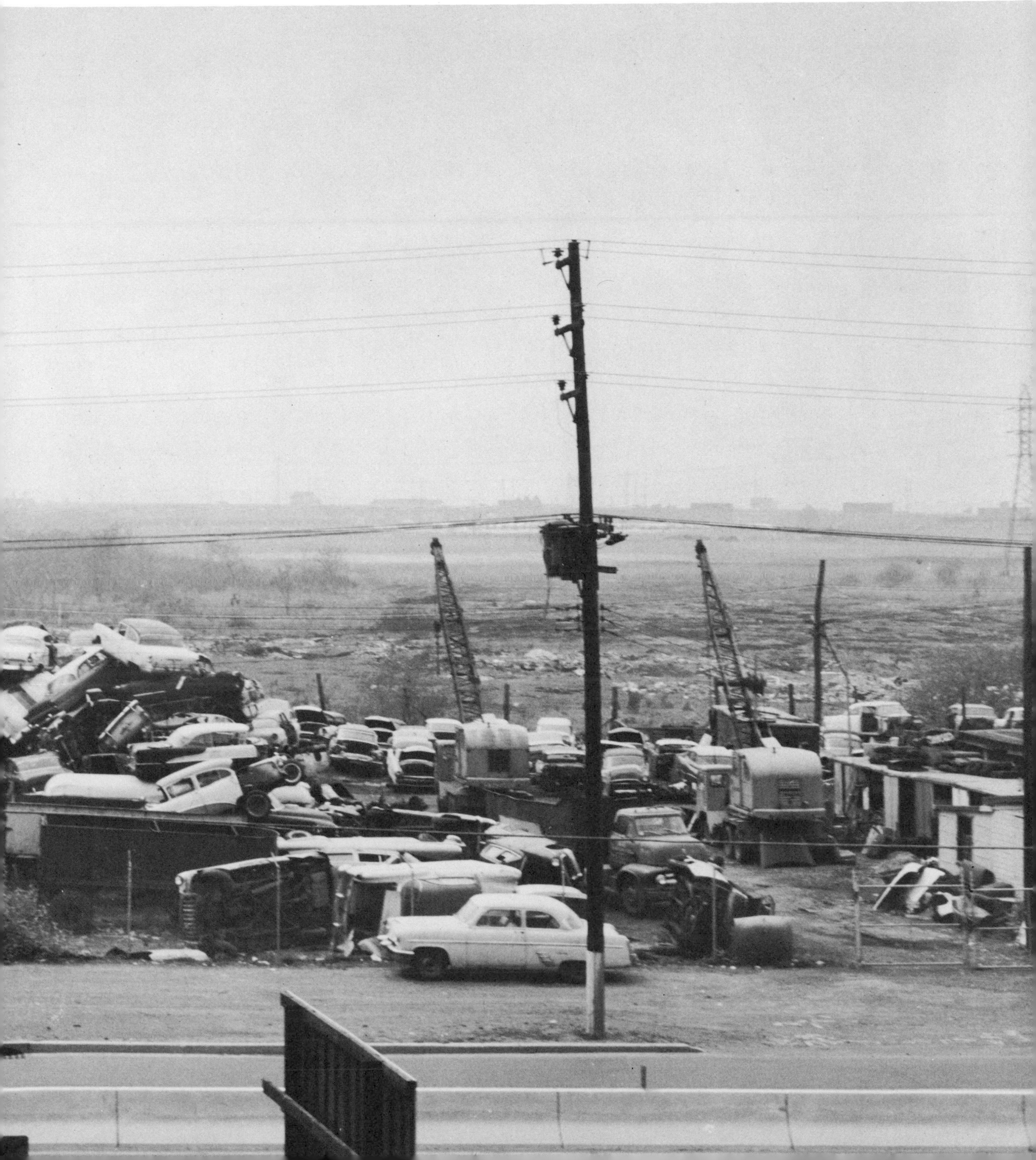

131

132

"The universe begins to look more like a great thought than like a great machine." SIR JAMES JEANS

Skyscape

Not long ago, an American housing expert, working in an "under-developed nation," suggested to his hosts that one way of reducing the cost of a new apartment project would be to string all the wiring overhead, rather than put it underground. His under-developed hosts were distinctly embarrassed. "You know," they said, "we've been putting our sewers and wiring and things like that underground for many years now. People just wouldn't accept having them up in the air."

In America, the most affluent nation of all, most of us do accept the cluttering up of the sky with wiring, TV aerials, roof tanks, billboards (including airborne billboards) and just about anything else that vulgarity or expediency can produce. We do so for the one reason that compels us to do so many things: it's cheaper—and what's the difference, anyway?

So the American skyline is not exactly a thing of beauty—the man-made skyline, that is: it boasts more light poles than trees; more tangled cables than branches, leaves or birds; more smog and soot than sun or stars. Where men once decorated their rooftops with gilded finials, we decorate ours with tar-papered watertanks, pipes, smoke stacks, vents, aerials, and illuminated billboards. Like children, we insist upon labeling most of our buildings, putting the name of the owner or tenant up on top in giant letters: one of the tallest, most prominently situated skyscrapers in the world, for example, is now crowned with the cryptic, mammoth words "PAN AM" (some sort of tribal chant, apparently) because the owners were persuaded by their publicity advisers that this giant badge was worth (exactly) $1 million per year in advertising! And yet we smile, a bit condescendingly, when we see the churches bearing signs that promise "JESUS SAVES" and similar good tidings.

It has been said that men are most Godlike when they create works of art, and that mankind has always exerted itself most nobly and creatively where its buildings reached toward the heavens—in domes, in spires, in campaniles. If our civilization, too, is to be known by the shapes of its upper extremities, then we will need all the saving that's available.

"A man can hardly lift up his eyes towards the heavens without wonder and veneration ..." SENECA

139

140 | 141

142 | 143

"By day or by night, summer or winter, beneath trees the heart feels nearer to that depth of life which the far sky means. The rest of spirit, found only in beauty, ideal and pure, comes there because the distance seems within touch of thought."
RICHARD JEFFERIES

147

*"Thank God, men cannot as yet fly, and
lay waste the sky as well as the earth!"*
HENRY DAVID THOREAU

155

156

"... enter this wild wood
And view the haunts of Nature. The calm shade
Shall bring a kindred calm; and the sweet breeze,
That makes the green leaves dance, shall waft a balm
To thy sick heart."
WILLIAM CULLEN BRYANT

To Determine That the Community Should be Beautiful

"It is within the power of the legislature to determine that the community should be beautiful. . . ." U.S. Supreme Court, November, 1954

When Supreme Court Justice William O. Douglas wrote the famous, unanimous court opinion in the case of *Berman versus Parker,** he may have gone a bit overboard. After all, who is to decide what is "beautiful"? How can beauty be legislated? And how could such legislation be enforced?

Still, the Supreme Court opinion in this case represents an impressive step forward, even if it is only a paper step. Granted that it is impossible to legislate beauty; still, the prerequisite for beauty—namely, a degree of order—can and should be legislated. But such legislation, like charity, begins at home; laws that do not reflect widespread popular consent cannot be enforced easily—as the Supreme Court knows only too well.

The trouble is, of course, that there is precious little popular consent or consensus in matters of beauty or in matters of order. Indeed, it can be shown rather convincingly that popular consensus today favors chaos.

The affluent society has many blessings, we are told, but it also contains within it the seeds of vandalism: for the first time in the history of mankind, we have complete and unrestricted freedom of esthetic choice! We can build anything, make anything, design anything, put it anywhere! Moreover, we can build, make, or design everything (so we tell ourselves) in such a way that it will be entirely different from everything else now extant on the face of the earth! The frantic search for novelty (for the sake of novelty) is encouraged by all the pressures that surround us: publications and other communications media are, by definition, dedicated to "news"; so that the successful writer, designer, musician, movie maker or artist is not the one who pursues quality, but the one who pursues and captures novelty.

An artist like the fifteenth-century Florentine sculptor, Lorenzo Ghiberti, who devoted most of his lifetime to the making of two pairs of bronze doors for the city's Duomo, would be quite unthinkable today: the insatiable hunger of the novelty seekers and the novelty peddlers requires that an artist change his technique or direction with every stroke of the brush, with every novel, with every building he designs. And the taste makers of museums or critical reviews are no different, in this respect, from the novelty peddlers of publications or advertising agencies: they, too, must unveil a new movement (or, at the very least, a new splinter group) every six months or every year.

All freedoms first lead to such abuses, of course: revolutions lead to indiscriminate bloodbaths—and our new, unlimited freedom of choice in material and esthetic things has led to indiscriminate vandalism. Yet the essence of all great art of all great periods of civilization has been the precise opposite: restraint, either self-imposed or, more frequently, imposed by economic or technical limitations.

Needless to say, it goes against the popular grain to suggest the imposition of limitations on freedom—especially on freedom of taste. In 1905, for example, a New Jersey court ruled in a billboard-control case (they had them even

---

* Excerpts from the court opinion: "Miserable and disreputable housing conditions may do more than spread disease and crime and immorality. They may also suffocate the spirit by reducing the people who live there to the status of cattle. They may indeed make living an almost insufferable burden. They may also be an ugly sore, a blight on the community which robs it of charm, which makes it a place from which men turn. . . . The concept of the public welfare is broad and inclusive. . . . The values it represents are spiritual as well as physical, aesthetic as well as monetary. It is within the power of the legislature to determine that the community should be beautiful as well as healthy, spacious as well as clean, well balanced as well as carefully patrolled . . .".

then!) that "aesthetic considerations are a matter of luxury and indulgence rather than of necessity"; and, more recently, the president of Outdoor Advertising, Inc., stated that "freedom to communicate is basic to our society, and . . . freedom of speech—freedom to be heard—also implies freedom to be seen. The right to communicate visually in the outdoor area . . . would seem to be one of our essential freedoms." Most Americans would probably agree.

It is easy enough to pretend that such views are held only by the thoughtless or the Philistines. This is not true. Precisely the same views, albeit couched in somewhat different language, are advanced by some of the most sophisticated artists in the land, and often with good reason: with the example, constantly before our eyes, of political control of the arts under all forms of dictatorship, artists and architects react instinctively against any real or imagined threat to their freedom of choice and of action. And most of them would react just as violently against "legislated beauty" as they have reacted against censorship of allegedly pornographic literature—not because these artists necessarily approve of billboards or of nudist magazines, but because they think it is not the state's business to intervene in such areas in any manner, shape or form.

This is an admirable position, but it oversimplifies the situation in several important respects.

Political and economic freedoms under democracy are (theoretically, at least) absolute—EXCEPT in so far as such freedoms are abused to limit the enjoyment of life, liberty, and the pursuit of happiness by our fellow men. This is obvious, of course: a citizen living in a democracy, under the rule of law, is expected to practice self-restraint in a great many ways. He cannot bump off his personal enemies because that would deprive them of their l., l., and p. of h.; he cannot drive his car through a red light (same reason), cheat his business partners, or, for that matter, build a rock-and-roll emporium next to a church in just about any city in the United States except Houston, Texas. In short, he is free as a lark so long as he does not impair the freedoms of his fellow men.

If and when this citizen in a democracy stops practicing self-restraint, governmental authority rears its ugly head. If and when a large number of citizens stops practicing self-restraint, the federal government may send troops to whereever it is that the citizenry has gone berserk. All of this is tacitly understood, at least in matters of conventional social, political, and economic behavior.

It is not so understood in matters of esthetic behavior. There is no doubt whatsoever that the l., l., and p. of h. of a considerable number of citizens are adversely affected by the organized (as well as haphazard) uglification of the United States. The evidence cited earlier of increased traffic accidents on billboarded highways, of mass protests against billboards and against the destruction of historically valuable buildings, and of terror in the streets of our mis-planned cities—all this could be added to, *ad infinitum*, by every reader of this book, from his or her personal experience. "The buildings along our streets belong to, and affect, all the people who use those streets," Professor Vincent Scully of Yale University said recently. The trouble with most of the eyesores created in America in recent years is that they are impossible to ignore.

Where any citizen is permitted a choice between degrading ugliness and beauty, the state has no right to step in and restrain the uglifier. No citizen is *forced* to look at "pop art," or listen to alleged musical compositions consisting of five simultaneously broadcast tape recordings of the mating calls of dromedaries, or watch supposedly prurient movies. He has a choice. **157**

But in America today, no citizen (except for an occasional hermit) has a chance to see anything but hideousness—all around him, day in and day out. We have more art schools than ever before, and more "art appreciation" courses; but how can a child in Gary, Indiana, say, be taught to use his eyes with discrimination, taste, and intelligence? How can he learn without being given a chance to compare? Where can he go even to look at a tree?

It is one of the best-loved popular misconceptions about the birth of the American republic that its fathers were "Men of the People." They were nothing of the sort, of course. They were aristocrats—at least intellectual aristocrats—who saw their mission as one of intellectual leadership.

Today, whenever architects, artists, writers, and critics gather to deplore, view with alarm, and write manifestos about the planned deterioration of America, there is much talk about hucksters and vulgarians and politicians and special interests. It is pretty good talk, and it is largely true talk—as far as it goes. But it misses one essential point: the point that the "intellectual elite" in America has failed miserably to accept its basic responsibilities, and to set an example for the rest of the country to follow—an example of self-imposed restraint, an example of quality rather than novelty.

It may be possible to create some degree of order in America—and, with it, a *chance* for civilization—by demanding such things as more stringent zoning laws, by taking the profit out of land speculation, by using tax policy to encourage good building and to discourage bad building, by ridding the country of the bureaucrats who have strait-jacketed most government-subsidized architecture, and by getting rid of their moribund agencies.

All this is essential; yet it is no more than preventive medicine. All this will do is *possibly* give us another chance.

But if we intend to do more—to create a great urban civilization in America, for example—then we need something in addition to more stringent laws and more effective controls over bureaucrats. We need creative acts; we need genuine leadership on the part of those capable of creating a new kind of city and a new kind of country.

At present, these should-be leaders are, instead, performing for Mr. Ripley's "Believe It or Not" circus: architects, painters, and sculptors are outdoing one another in acrobatics, in hot pursuit of novelty; taste makers are busy watching the box office and the circulation figures, instead of making taste; and the public (which includes the public uglifiers) simply follows the lead of our supposed "intellectual elite."

For the truth is that the mess that is man-made America is merely a caricature of the mess that is art in America—and a very mild caricature at that. The inscription on Sir Christopher Wren's tomb in St. Paul's Cathedral contains the famous words: "If thou seek his monument, look about thee." God forbid that this should ever become *our* epitaph. . . .

All photographs not otherwise credited are by the author.

1. University of Virginia, by Thomas Jefferson. Photo: George Cserna.
2. Canal Street, New Orleans. Photo: Wallace Litwin.
3. Times Square, New York City.
4. Miami Beach.
5. Smithsonian Institution, Washington, D.C. Photo: John Burwell.
6. Times Square centerpiece, New York City.
7. Miami Beach.
8. The Mall, Washington, D.C. Photo: Yoichi R. Okamoto.
9. Town Hall, Owego, N.Y.
10. Miami Beach.
11. Monument in Miami. Photo: Miami-Metro News Bureau.
12. Housing in New York City. Photo: Kerry A. Mayer.
13. Hosuing in Washington, D.C. Photo: George Cserna.
14. Salt Lake City, Utah. Photo: Rondal Partridge.
15. Beacon Hill, Boston. Photo: Clemens Kalischer.
16. Public Library, New York City. Photo: Chester (Black Star).
17. Miami Beach.
18. New York City skyline.
19. New York City skyline.
20. Vista in Washington, D.C.
21. Jackson, Miss. Photo: Marion Cost Wolcott (Courtesy, Library of Congress).
22. Bridgehampton, N.Y.
23. Custom House and neighbor, New York City.
24. Park Avenue in 1949 (looking south). Photo: Courtesy, General Electric Co.
25. Same view in 1963.
26. Park Avenue in 1943 (looking north). Photo: Acme Photo.
27. Same view in 1963.
28. Detroit highways. Photo: Elliott Erwitt (Magnum).
29. Detroit highways. Photo: Elliott Erwitt (Magnum).
30. Detroit highways. Photo: Elliott Erwitt (Magnum).
31. Boston expressway. Photo: Courtesy, Architectural Forum.
32. New Jersey highways. Photo: Courtesy, Standard Oil Co. (N.J.)
33. Detroit highways. Photo: Elliott Erwitt (Magnum).
34. Store in San Francisco. Photo: Rondal Partridge.
35. Store in New York City. Photo: Bernard Liebman.
36. Store in New Mexico. Photo: Russell Lee (Courtesy, Library of Congress).
37. Showrooms in Manhattan.
38. Restaurant in Manhattan.
39. Store on Long Island, N.Y.
40. Back street in Chicago.
41. Beacon Hill, Boston. Photo: Clemens Kalischer.
42. Suburb near Chicago. Photo: Luree's Photo Service.
43. Suburb near Detroit. Photo: Balthazar.
44. West Village, New York City. Photo: Carter Winter.
45. Suburb in New Jersey.
46. Suburb in Pennsylvania.
47. Suburb in Texas. Photo: Reeves.
48. Row houses in Washington, D.C. Photo: Robert C. Lautman.
49. Contra Costa County, California. Photo: Rondal Partridge.
50. Highway 64, Arizona. Photo: Rondal Partridge.
51. Three Forks, Montana. Photo: Arthur Rothstein (Courtesy, Library of Congress).
52. Northern Wisconsin. Photo: John Vachon (Courtesy, Library of Congress).
53. Wisconsin. Photo: John Vachon (Courtesy, Library of Congress).
54. Ducktown, Tennessee. Photo: Marion Post Wolcott (Courtesy, Library of Congress).
55. Marion, Virginia. Photo: Marion Post Wolcott (Courtesy, Library of Congress).
56. Greene County, Louisiana. Photo: Marion Post Wolcott (Courtesy, Library of Congress).
57. Nevada desert. Photo: Arthur Rothstein (Courtesy, Library of Congress).
58. Highway 66 near Flagstaff, Arizona. Photo: Phil Stitt.
59. Willamette National Forest, Oregon. Photo: Russell Lee (Courtesy, Library of Congress).
60. Near Oneonta, New York. Photo: New York State Department of Commerce.
61. Ducktown, Tennessee. Photo: John Vachon (Courtesy, Library of Congress).
62. Old Doheny Ranch, California. Photo: Spence Air Photos.
63. Contra Costa County, California. Photo: Rondal Partridge.
64. Trousdale Estates, California. Photo: Pacific Air Industries.
65. Grant County, Oregon. Photo: Russell Lee (Courtesy, Library of Congress).
66. Connecticut beach. Photo: Scaylea (Courtesy, Connecticut Development Commission).
67. California beach. Photo: William M. Graham (Photo Researchers Inc.).
68. Columbus, Georgia. Photo: Jack Delano (Courtesy, Library of Congress).
69. Surfside Way, Nantucket. Photo: Nantucket Island Chamber of Commerce.
70. Long Beach Island, New Jersey.
71. Montauk Point, New York. Photo: New York State Department of Commerce.
72. Miami Beach. Photo: Wallace Litwin.
73. Hawaii. Photo: Ernest Gay.
74. Hawaii. Photo: Ernest Gay.
75. Trailer camp in Colorado.
76. Sierra landscape, California. Photo: Rondal Partridge.
77. Glacier National Park, Montana. Photo: Marion Post Wolcott (Courtesy, Library of Congress).
78. Miami Beach hotel and pool.
79. Giant sequoia, California. Photo: Marc Riboud (Magnum).

80. Forest in Black River, Wisconsin. Photo: Russell Lee (Courtesy, Library of Congress).
81. Fort Lee, New Jersey.
82. Allison Park, New Jersey.
83. Hicksville, Long Island, New York, 1945. Photo: Fairchild Aerial Surveys.
84. "Levittown," or Hicksville, ten years later. Photo: Fairchild Aerial Surveys.
85. Elmont, Long Island, New York, 1945. Photo: Fairchild Aerial Surveys.
86. Elmont, Long Island, ten years later. Photo: Fairchild Aerial Surveys.
87. Subdivision near Oakland, California. Photo: Clyde Sunderland—Oakland.
88. Automobile graveyard near Detroit. Photo: Elliott Erwitt (Magnum).
89. Hackensack River Valley, New Jersey.
90. American landscape. Photo: Cartier-Bresson (Magnum).
91. Plainview, Long Island, New York. Photo: Peter Roll (Photo Researchers).
92. Arlington Cemetery, Virginia. Photo: Inger Abrahamsen (Rapho Guillumette).
93. Miami Beach marina. Photo: Wallace Litwin.
94. Sailboats on Long Island. Photo: Hans Namuth.
95. San Francisco Municipal Pier. Photo: Rondal Partridge.
96. Rockport, Maine. Photo: Norton (Courtesy, Maine Department of Economic Development).
97. Lake Minnewaska, New York. Photo: New York State Department of Commerce.
98. Worth County, Iowa. Photo: Arthur Rothstein (Courtesy, Library of Congress).
99. Suburban development near Detroit. Photo: Balthazar.
100. Highway sign, Ohio. Photo: Ben Shahn (Courtesy, Library of Congress).
101. Roadside stand, Long Island.
102. Greenbelt, Maryland. Photo: Marion Post Wolcott (Courtesy, Library of Congress).
103. Minneapolis park. Photo: John Vachon (Courtesy, Library of Congress).
104, 105, 106, 107. Subdivision under construction, near Los Angeles. Photos: William Garnett.
108. Merritt Parkway, Connecticut. Photo: Standard Oil Co. (N.J.).
109. Camden, New Jersey. Photo: Standard Oil Co. (N.J.).
110. Natchez, Mississippi. Photo: Marion Post Wolcott (Courtesy, Library of Congress).
111. Highway 66, California. Photo: Rondal Partridge.
112. After a "Bean Day Festival," New Mexico. Photo: Russell Lee (Courtesy, Library of Congress).
113. Highway 66, Arizona. Photo: Rondal Partridge.
114. New Mexico landscape. Photo: Courtesy *The New Mexico Architect.*
115. Washington-Baltimore Expressway.
116. Miami Beach, Florida. Photo: Wallace Litwin.
117. New Jersey parking lot.
118. Road in Pennsylvania. Photo: Marion Post Wolcott (Courtesy, Library of Congress).
119. Highway 66, California. Photo: Rondal Partridge.
120. Lover's Lane, Washington, D.C. Photo: George Cserna.
121. Abbeville, Louisiana, junkyard. Photo: Russell Lee (Courtesy, Library of Congress).
122. Highway 99, California. Photo: Dorothea Lange (Courtesy, Library of Congress).
123. Main Street, Long Island. Photo: Berenice Abbott.
124. Post Office Department, Washington, D.C. Photo: Courtesy, Architectural Forum.
125. Auto graveyard, Arkansas. Photo: George Wolfe (Courtesy, Library of Congress).
126. Parking lot, Long Island shore. Photo: Cornell Capa (Magnum).
127. Headlights, 1963 style.
128. Hackensack River Valley, New Jersey.
129. Near Bridgeton, New Jersey. Photo: Edwin Rosekam (Courtesy, Library of Congress).
130. Scrap pile, Butte, Montana. Photo: Russell Lee (Courtesy, Library of Congress).
131. Valley in Colorado.
132. Scene near Kilgore, Texas. Photo: Russell Lee (Courtesy, Library of Congress).
133. Trees along Bronx River Parkway, New York. Photo: Standard Oil Co. (N.J.).
134. Telephone poles, Richmond, California. Photo: Rondal Partridge.
135. Subdivision display, Irving, Texas. Photo: Shel Hershorn.
136. 42nd Street, New York City.
137. Flying swans, Suffolk County, New York.
138. Trees along Fox River, Illinois. Photo: George H. Steuer.
139, 140, 141, 142, 143. Telephone and light poles, New York, New Jersey, and Pennsylvania.
144. Contra Costa landscape, California. Photo: Rondal Partridge.
145. Navajo Reservation, Arizona. Photo: Rondal Partridge.
146. Power lines, New Jersey.
147. El Camino Real, Palo Alto, California. Photo: Rondal Partridge.
148. Eighth Avenue, New York City.
149. Seventh Avenue, New York City.
150. Colorado skyline, Denver.
151. Spring Green, Wisconsin. Photo: Ezra Stoller.
152. Airship advertising movies. Photo: Acme-U.P.I.
153. Airborne advertisment. Photo: UPI.
154. Goodyear blimps over New York Harbor. Photo: Acme-UPI.
155. Telephone poles, Cincinnati. Photo: Fred Eichenhofer.
156. Pole and stop sign, Maryland.
157. Winter scene, Ithaca, New York.